POSTMODERN CHRISTIANITY
AND THE RECONSTRUCTION OF
THE CHRISTIAN MIND

James P. Danaher

POSTMODERN CHRISTIANITY AND THE RECONSTRUCTION OF THE CHRISTIAN MIND

by
James P. Danaher

Academica Press, LLC
Bethesda, Dublin, London
2001

Library of Congress Cataloging-in-Publication Data
(Applied for April 28, 2001)

Editorial Inquiries:
Academica Press, LLC
7831 Woodmont Avenue, #381
Bethesda, MD 20814
Website: www.academicapress.com
To order: (202)388-1800

Contents

vi

for my wife, Kathy

Acknowledgments

I would like to especially thank Professor Charles Beach whose invaluable recommendations and suggestions have greatly enhanced this project.

I would also like to acknowledge that much of the material that makes up the chapters of this text had previously appeared in modified versions in several philosophy and theology journals. I would like to thank the following journals for allowing me to reproduce that work here: *The Asbury Theological Journal, Ashland Theological Journal, Bridges, Contemporary Philosophy, Encounter, The European Journal of Theology, Evangel, Lexington Theological Quarterly, The Philosopher, Philosophia Christi, Philosophical Inquiry, Science and Christian Belief, Sophia, Southwest Philosophy Review,* and *Theology Today.*

Chapter 1

Introduction

Much has been made recently concerning gender differences and their effect upon communication between men and women. It is argued, both in the popular literature (e.g., Gray's, *Men are from Mars, Women are from Venus*) as well as the more scholarly literature (e.g., Tannen's, *You Just Don't Understand: Women and Men in Conversation*), that communication between women and men is hampered by the fact that their respective cultural experiences are so different. In spite of these differences which hamper communication between the sexes, the literature holds out hope that communication is possible if we come to acknowledge and understand these differences.

If gender differences affect communication between the sexes, then there must be enormous difficulties in communication between God and man. Of course, in that God is all knowing, our communication to him is not hampered. Since he knows all things, our intentional meaning does not escape his understanding. However, in so far as God's intentional meaning did not originate out of any culture or experience even remotely resembling anything human, there is an inherent estrangement between his intentional meaning and our understanding.

Today, the fact that our conceptual understanding (or at least a large portion of it) is relative to our language community and culture is undeniable. By contrast, God's conceptual understanding is not the product of any human language community or culture, and so may be very different from our own. If God wished to communicate to human beings, whatever words he would choose would signify to us concepts of a human language community. Such concepts may not reflect God's intentional meaning.

Given such a situation, God could, of course, still communicate to human beings on a certain level. He could, for instance, give us simple commands or communicate information that did not require that we conceptualize as he does, just as we communicate to lower animals. But it would seem that what he could not do is express his intentional meaning, since the concepts that human words signify are not God's concepts but those of human language communities. Of course, in communicating to human beings God would choose words that signify an intentional meaning as close as possible to his own. Some have argued that this is why it is best to study Scripture in the original ancient languages rather than modern translations, since those languages must have been chosen because they more closely signify God's intentional meaning. There may be some truth to this, but the study of ancient languages does not necessarily bring us any closer to God's intentional meaning: it only reproduces the problem in another language community and culture. The problem is that even though ancient Greek or Hebrew might, on average, have concepts which more closely replicate God's intentional meaning, it is not immediately obvious which human words signify concepts very close to God's intentional meaning, and which, although remote, are the closest that a human language has to what he wishes to express. Without some means to know which are the tight fits and which are the loose fits, it is difficult to know how to interpret God's intentional meaning.

Of course, some would argue that the problem I am setting forth commits the intentional fallacy. They would claim that it is a mistake to attempt to interpret a piece of literature (in this case the Bible) from the perspective of the author's intentional meaning. There is certainly some merit to this criticism when dealing with literature produced by human authors, but the two major supports of the intentional fallacy collapse if the author is divine rather than human.

The first support of the intentional fallacy is that much of what human authors produce may be the result of the author's unconscious, and therefore the meaning of the text goes beyond the meaning that the author was aware of or consciously intended. Of course, if the divine mind is all knowing, then his omniscience extends to the infinite recess of his own understanding. An omniscient mind cannot contain an unconscious.

The second support of the intentional fallacy is that our desire to know the author's intentional meaning can take us away from the text itself and cause us to delve into the life and circumstances of the author. This too is a criticism with merit concerning human authors, but if the author is a transcendent God, the criticism is unfounded since no biographical circumstances exist apart from the text.

Furthermore, if a divine, transcendent author wished to make himself known in an intimate and personal way through a text (which is certainly a possibility that must remain open) then the intentional meaning of such an author is all important.

Certainly there are barriers to the communication of such intentional meaning, and there is a natural estrangement between God and human beings, but the situation is not hopeless, and man's natural estrangement from God's conceptual understanding may be overcome. Perhaps this estrangement may not be overcome to the degree we would like, and our conceptual understanding will never completely replicate God's, but it is possible for our concepts to become a little less human and a little more divine.

After a brief explanation of how such a problem can be solved by first understanding our natural estrangement, and then using the instances of Scripture as extensions of the concepts that God wishes to communicate, subsequent chapters give examples of how we might reconstruct some of our key concepts in order that they might better reflect God's intentional meaning. These subsequent chapters also address obstacles in our thinking which prevent, or at least hamper, our understanding of God's concepts. Some of these obstacles include the fact that our cultural tradition in the west, especially since the time of Enlightenment, has been toward ever more narrow and precise concepts after the model of mathematics. By contrast, the biblical instances offer extensions of concepts much broader and richer than those of our culture. Equally, some concepts are extremely difficult to communicate because there are no instances in this world which might serve as extensions of those concepts. Still other concepts which the biblical instances attempt to communicate are difficult because they are contrary to certain basic, cultural concepts concerning how we think. All of these difficulties come down to the fact that our concepts are tainted by a culture and perspective that are all-too-human.

This book is an attempt to break down some of that cultural veneer. It is both postmodern and conservative in that it embraces and endorses a postmodern perspective but, at the same time, suggests a solution to the problem created by that perspective that is both biblical and conservative.

Chapter 2

Postmodern Hermeneutics

Christians may disagree with what many postmodern authors offer as an alternative to modernity, but the postmodern criticism of modernity seems well founded. Essentially, postmodernism, as a general opposition to modernity, argues that the cornerstones of modernity, which include a materialist and mechanical view of nature, and the belief that we can know such a reality objectively and in a quantifiably precise way, are both unrealistic and undesirable. This attack on modernity that has come to be known as postmodernism is not new, and modernity has had its critics from the start. Certainly the romantic poets of the eighteenth and nineteenth centuries were among these critics, but there were strains of opposition within many philosophers as well. Berkeley and Leibniz opposed the materialist, mechanical view of modernity, while Locke, Hume, and Kant questioned our ability to know the world objectively. But apart from the academy, little attention was paid to such critics. The apparent unparalleled progress which the modern worldview claimed to have produced made any criticism seem pedantic. By the end of the twentieth century, however, many have reassessed that progress and found the human condition in a state much worse than the prophets of modernity had promised. Additionally, science has continued to produce evidence that makes the materialist, mechanical worldview ever more unrealistic. The world is more complex than the model of modernity allows, and our understanding of it is never objective but always subjective and relative to our language community and culture.

This fact that our understanding is relative to our language community and culture has significance to Christians because it means that the words put forth in Scripture signify concepts that are the products of human language communities and, as such, reflect the judgments of human beings rather than God's intentional meaning. Thus, there is a natural estrangement between human beings and God. Beyond the fact that we have sinned and fallen short of the glory of God, we also experience an estrangement in our understanding since the concepts by which our understanding is organized and arranged are largely the product of our language communities and cultures. Since God's understanding is not the product of any human language community, his understanding may be considerably different from our own. When God speaks to us through human language, as he does in Scripture, the words he uses will signify to us the concepts those words signify in our language communities and not necessarily God's intentional meaning. The problem is that our conceptualization of the world is "all too human."

Of course, we do have some sort of God-given mental hardware that allows us to form concepts, and it is possible that this hardware universally prevents us from conceiving some things other than we do. Equally, the nature of some experiences may be such that alternative conceptual judgments are not possible, and in that case, our understanding is not culturally relative. In spite of these facts, however, the postmodern insight that our understanding is "all too human" seems undeniable, for in addition to whatever natural equipping we may have to universally form certain concepts, we also have been given an enormous freedom to conceptualize most of our experience in a variety of ways.

This freedom can easily be seen in children as they begin to acquire language. Their earliest concepts are often different from those that their language community associates with a particular signifier or word. The first concept a child might form and identify with the word *dog* might be a general notion that includes many kinds of pets, or it may be very narrow and include characteristics peculiar to the child's own dog. It is only as more instances of the signifier *dog* are identified that the child's concept becomes something close to that of the language community. Thus, with their exposure to language, children's initial freedom to form concepts becomes restricted, and their concepts are molded and come to conform to those held by the language community. Such conformity, however, is not toward some absolute understanding which represents objective reality. Instead, the signification that our language community attaches to a particular word is arbitrary, at least in the sense that there exists an enormous number of alternative ways that we could group our experiences. Although our perceptual reality may be based upon an objective physical world, our conceptual reality is based largely upon the various ways our language community and culture have come to divide up the world.

Given this fact, the meaning we attribute to whatever words God might communicate to us would reflect the concepts of our culture rather than God's intentional meaning. For instance, Jesus says, "Love your neighbor as yourself" (Matt. 19:19 NIV). Of course, our understanding of *neighbor*, or even our understanding of a human being, is culturally and historically relative. Certainly the Klansman conceives of people of other races as less than human. But such cultural relativism is not confined to small out-groups. Indeed, nineteenth century American culture at large held a similar view as witnessed by the Dred Scott decision.

My personal belief is that God has no concept of race at all; nevertheless, our culture has chosen to distinguish black people from white people, and we form concepts that allow for such a distinction. In fact, however, an almost infinite variety of other races could be established based on an equally infinite variety of characteristics. Our concepts of black people and white people are the result of a choice to form one specific notion of race rather than some other.

With diseases it is equally easy to see that the essential characteristics we select to form our concepts are obviously nominal and the product of judgments rather than any God-given ability to correctly organize our experience. But if our concepts of things like races and diseases are nominal and of our own creation, then all, or nearly all, of our concepts are suspect. In order for us to claim any of our concepts as natural or God-given, we need to show why we believe they are more than nominal and the product of more than mere human judgment and convention. Without a criterion to separate nominal from natural (or God-given) concepts, they all must be treated as nominal, and thus conceptual reality must be understood as a linguistic and cultural construct.

Consequently, we are forced to accept a healthy skepticism regarding "exactly" what God is intending to communicate. But this skepticism is not to be lamented. Indeed, it seems an appropriate prescription for our human condition. Without such a skepticism toward God's exact, intentional meaning, we naively suppose that the judgments of our culture are God-given. Without such skepticism, we all too easily believe that God, rather than our culture, gave us our concepts of black people and white people, schizophrenia and mid-life crisis. Without such skepticism, we all too easily believe that our ideas of good and evil are God-given rather than largely the product of human judgment passed on to us by our culture. Without a skepticism concerning God's concepts, I come to believe that there is no better way to understand the world because my understanding replicates God's understanding. Such a confident knowing has always bred brutal intolerance and prevents God from bringing us to an ever greater understanding. By contrast, being free from the belief that we have a natural ability to know God's concepts humbles us and brings us to the truth that God has

> afforded us only the twilight, as I may so say, of <u>Probability</u>, suitable, I
> presume, to that State of Mediocrity and Probationership, he has been pleased
> to place us in here; wherein to check our over-confidence and presumption, we
> might by every day's Experience be made sensible of our short-sightedness and
> liableness to Error; the Sense whereof might be a constant Admonition to us,
> to spend the days of this our Pilgrimage with Industry and Care, in search, and
> following of that way, which might lead us to a State of greater Perfection.
> (Locke IV. xiv. 2)

More importantly, however, than being able to "check our over-confidence and presumption," and "be a constant Admonition to us," and reminder "of our short-sightedness and liableness to Error," a skepticism concerning a knowledge of God's understanding is the necessary first step, if we are to have our concepts reformed and our minds renewed in order to reflect God's intentional meaning. Such a reformation and renewal must begin by understanding our natural estrangement from God's conceptual understanding. Unless we understand that there is initially something wrong with our understanding, it is impossible even to begin the process by which our concepts might be reformed and our minds renewed.

After this first step of realizing our natural estrangement from God's understanding, the second step is to understand something about the nature of concepts themselves. Particularly, we need to understand that the ancients were wrong in their thinking about concepts. For the most part, the ancients believed that concepts were what cause particular instances to be grouped together into species or kinds, and therefore, since they are the basis for instances being grouped into kinds, they must precede the collection of the instances. In truth, however, the opposite is usually the case. As we have seen, children acquire concepts as they are exposed to language. As more and more instances are identified by the same signifier, the child begins to form a mental representation and associates it with that particular signifier or word. With the addition of more instances, the mental representation becomes refined until it replicates something close to what is held by the language community.

If this is how a concept is formed, then what we need in order to have a knowledge of God's concepts is not some innate ability to know as God knows, but rather sets of instances that God sets forth as extensions of his concepts. Of course, we have just such sets of instances provided by Scripture. Although Scripture may be of little use concerning many of the concepts on which we would like to have a divine perspective, it does provide us with enough instances of certain important spiritual and moral concepts to allow us to form mental representations of our own which more accurately approximate God's understanding. Since the instances provided by Scripture are God-given and usually quite different from those provided by our language community, we have a basis from which to form more godly concepts than those we acquired from our culture in our acquisition of language. Because we have an inherent freedom to create concepts by grouping particular instances in a variety of ways, we are free to create new ones and reform old ones by choosing to form our concepts according to the instances that Scripture provides. Thus, in spite of the fact that we have little natural ability to know God-given concepts beyond that which is part of our linguistic or mental hardware, we are able to avoid an absolute skepticism concerning God's conceptual understanding because we do have biblical instances which serve as extensions of some of God's most important concepts. From the instances provided by Scripture, we have a basis upon which to reform our concepts and renew our minds in a way that reflects God's conceptual understanding.

This reformation of our concepts occurs much in the same way that we originally formed our concepts. Originally, our concept *dog* may have indicated a four-legged sock-eater, but as we experienced more instances signified by the same signifier, our concept changed. Not all instances to which the signifier *dog* was attached involved sock-eaters, and there were many more things that had four legs than were signified by the word *dog*. Our notion *dog* changed to accommodate the instances signified by other speakers of our language community. If we had been presented with a different set of instances, they would have produced a different concept within us. With the Scriptures we have such a different set of instances which are capable of producing in us concepts different from those which our culture originally forced upon us through the acquisition of language.

Thus, the Scripture truly is capable of communicating many of God's most important concepts if we are willing to "be not fashioned according to this world," but are willing to be "transformed by the renewing of [our] mind" (Rom. 12.2 KJV). There is nothing new in this, and God's people have long been using Scripture in just such a way. All that is necessary is to recognize that in many cases our concepts are very different than God's, and that Scripture is capable of renewing our minds after God's understanding. The way this reformation of our minds occurs is not unlike the way our minds were initially equipped in our first exposure to language. Hence, we must become as babes and allow the biblical instances to recreate our concepts just as we allowed the instances provided by our language communities to originally form our concepts.

It is also necessary, however, to understand that the concepts that God wishes to communicate to us are fundamentally different than those of human language communities. God's concepts are not common or the product of a community, nor did God acquire them in the same manner that we acquired our concepts.

The idea that concepts can be of different kinds is not new. Wittgenstein understood that there were different kinds of concepts. Unlike Plato and nearly the entire Western tradition that followed him, Wittgenstein realized that language, and its concepts, functions differently in different situations, and for different purposes (*Blue and Brown* 1). This is largely due to the fact that human beings, and their language, function on several levels, and thus so do their concepts. Wittgenstein says that we can create exact concepts for specific purposes and that these stand as additions to those that we use for common language (*Philosophical Investigations* sects. 68-69). In addition to the common notion of "water" which I communicate in order to satisfy my thirst, there may also be an exact concept of "H2O" which allows me to communicate a more precise meaning of the same signifier or word. But although Wittgenstein acknowledges different kinds of concepts, he denies that there can be a private language with words which refer to concepts or inner experiences that are totally private and only known to an individual *(Philosophical Investigations* sects. 243-315). Language, for Wittgenstein, is always common and the product of a community. His arguments against the idea of a private language are convincing, but such arguments remain on a purely human level and do not bring God into the mix. Not that God has a language that is knowable only to himself, but certainly God's concepts are not the product of any language community, and their origins are purely personal rather than common. By contrast, if all of our concepts are common, as Wittgenstein argues, then how could we ever know such divine concepts that are so different in kind from our own? Are such concepts, which are so different from our own, even imaginable?

I believe they are imaginable and even knowable. My reason for believing this is that we too have concepts that are very different from those of our language community. Indeed, in addition to the concepts given us by our language communities, we also have concepts which, like God's, originate privately and are not the product of a language community. Not that they are part of a private language known only to each individual, but they are concepts that are personal, and not common or the product of a community. Our first concept of *dog* began as a personal concept. Of course, it was molded into a common notion, but it began as a personal or private one. Additionally, we retain many concepts that are not the product of our language community but are private and the result of our own personal experience and judgment. For example, in addition to my common concept of water and the more scientific notion of H_2O, there is also a concept of water that represents the stuff I played in as a child. This is not what I commonly communicate, but it is what I often wish to communicate in my more intimate communions where I wish to express more private or personal meanings. This personal concept is different from what the language community commonly holds. It is my private concept of *water* which has a distinct meaning only to me, but it is nevertheless what I sometimes wish to communicate to another human being, usually someone with whom I am intimate.

On the common level, or even the precise scientific level, a concept is little more than a commonly understood boundary that separates particular things into one kind or another, on the more personal level, however, a concept is really not common at all. Plato's idea of an *eidos* or what is common to all members of a species only applies to the common or scientific notions and omits completely the idea of a personal concept (*Meno* 72A-79E). Personal concepts are different from their common or scientific counterpart in that they are not known in abstraction but from the perspective of a person. When they are communicated to me, what I grasp is not something common by something personal.

In common communication, we use concepts for the purpose of utility, and knowing the intentional meaning of a speaker is not important, but at other times when we wish to communicate for the purpose of intimacy, the intentional meaning of the speaker is important. Equally, with common communication, the concept is most often used as a means to identify the extensions of that concept, but when we wish to share our intentional meanings in more intimate communication, we generally use instances or extensions as the means, and the purpose is to communicate the concept itself. Of course, an exact communication of such an intentional meaning is impossible, but the purpose of this kind of personal communication is not to establish the kind of exactness sought in the sciences but to intimately share with another person the way one distinctively conceptualizes the world.

With human beings, personal concepts may begin as common concepts acquired through language, but because they become of particular interest and importance to us, we attach additional meaning and significance to them. Such concepts often more genuinely define us than our occupations or social status, and they are what we want others to know about us. Such concepts represent the objects of our greatest interest and affection. The person who loves dogs has a different notion of those animals than other members of the language community. He is familiar with the common notion, but his concept includes things that the one who is not a dog lover would have difficulty imagining. Similarly, the person whose interest is money has a concept of money that goes far beyond what others signify by the same word.

Ortega y Gasset says:

> In truth, nothing characterizes us as much as our field of attention . . . This formula might well be accepted: tell me where your attention lies and I will tell you who you are. (Ortega y Gasset 26)

This is certainly true, but our field of attention is always conceptually constructed. It is not what we perceive that makes something important to us, but how we conceive it. More than our fingerprints, the things that most truly identify and personalize us are those personal concepts which we have given much time and attention to develop. Equally, these are often the things we are most attracted to in another person.

The way in which personal concepts are communicated is similar to the way common concepts are communicated to us in our initial exposure to language. As we saw earlier, a child's concept may begin as something distinctly different from that of her language community. It is shaped, however, as additional instances of a given signifier or word are provided. With the additional instances, eventually the child's concept becomes something close to that which is held by the language community at large. Likewise, the same is true regarding the communication of our personal concepts, with the exception that with them there is a single instructor concerning the correct extension of the concept.

The other distinction concerning our communication of personal rather than common concepts lies in the fact that we communicate one for the sake of intimacy and the other for the sake of a variety of reasons other than intimacy. Indeed, personal concepts are usually communicated in our most intimate relationships. In a marriage, one way spouses intimately communicate to their mates is by expressing the distinctive intentional meaning they assign to a certain important concept. The first step in such communication is for the spouses to convince their mates that what they mean by a certain signifier is not what is commonly meant, and that the concept to which a signifier commonly or even scientifically refers is of little use in trying to understand their personal concept. Without understanding our natural estrangement from the personal concepts of others, we will never even begin to enter into communication on this more personal level.

After my wife has convinced me that I do not understand a particular concept that is important and peculiar to her, she then gives instances of what she does mean. As she sets out additional instances, I come ever closer to an understanding of her intentional meaning, just as I had through a similar process come to understand the public meaning referenced by that word. The main difference lies in the fact that the private or personal concept is much more complex and includes many more aspects peculiar to my wife's experiences, judgments, and values. These particular aspects would certainly be eliminated from the public concept of that same word or signifier.

In order to know my wife intimately, I need to know how she particularly conceptualizes those things that are most important to her. I begin by understanding that I am not naturally equipped to know her most important concepts. I equally have to be willing to come to know them, and she needs to instruct me concerning instances which might serve as extensions of them.

Since we ourselves have the capacity to form private concepts that are different from those of our language community, and we are able to express these private concepts by using the common concepts of our language community, it should not be surprising that God can do the same. Just as in the case with my wife, in order for me to know God intimately, I need to know how he particularly conceptualizes those things that are most important to him. I need to begin by understanding that I am not naturally equipped with an understanding of his intentional meaning. Equally, I have to desire to know his concepts, and finally he has to instruct me concerning the proper extensions of them.

In Scripture, we have the kind of instruction we need to point out the correct extensions of God's most important concepts. The instances the Bible offers of things like love and faith provide extensions of God's concepts, and thus we can come to understand his intentional meaning, just as we can come to understand our spouses' intentional meaning through the instances they provide as extensions of their important personal concepts.

In spite of the fact that our language communities impose their concepts upon us, we are nevertheless free to form personal concepts and communicate them to others, and we do so by using conventional language and its common concepts. Philosophers in particular create new concepts out of their particular experience and judgment, and they communicate them to others using existing language and its common concepts. Sometimes a philosopher may invent a new word to signify a new concept, but a new word is not necessary, and new concepts can be expressed using existing words. All that is necessary is that they give instances which serve as extensions of the new concept.

The same is, of course, true of God. He can communicate his unique concept of something like "love" through the biblical instances which serve as extensions of his concept. Today, the word *agape* signifies what we believe to be God's concept of love, but the word did not have that meaning when the Bible was being written. At that time, the word *agape* signified a broad and common concept of love. Indeed, the biblical concept of *agape* love did not exist before the biblical instances that created it.

Contrary to the common notion, the New Testament does not designate a particularly divine kind of love with the word, *agape*. Nor does the New Testament reserve the word *philia* for that less than divine affection which is so common among human beings. Of course, there are times when *philia* does seem to designate a worldly type of affection, but in other places *philia* looks like godly affection. Statements such as "For the Father *loves* the son" (John 5:20 NIV) or "the Father himself *loves* you because you have loved me" (John 16:27 NIV) certainly seem to be examples of godly rather than human affection, but in both cases the Greek *philia* is used.

The same is true regarding *agape*. At times it does seem to connote the special, divine kind of affection of which Jesus so often speaks, but at other times it refers to common human affection. Statements such as "Woe to you Pharisees, because you *love* the most important seats in the synagogues" (Luke 11:43 NIV), "Light has come into the world, but men *loved* darkness instead of light" (John 3:19 NIV), "they *loved* praise from men more than praise from God" (John 12:43 NIV), or "Do not *love* the world or anything in the world" (1 John 2:15 NIV) are all instances of *love* translated from the Greek word *agape,* and all are examples of something far less than the special sort of divine love that we are told *agape* is supposed to signify.

The truth is that *agape* was simply a common Greek word for affection, and the writers of Scripture used it to refer to a broad variety of types of affection. Since, however, Jesus, and later the disciples, often spoke of a new and radically different kind of affection, we sought, for the sake of our own understanding, to designate a word to refer specifically to that particular concept of New Testament love. Today we designate *agape* as that word, but this designation of *agape* is not to be found in Scripture or the early church. Thus, the fact that the words God uses to communicate to us do not signify his concepts, but rather those of our language community, does not prevent God from expressing his intentional meaning to us.

This should be obvious since we too are able to express our peculiar intentional meaning to others in spite of the fact that the concepts we often wish to express are different from the common concepts of our language community. All that is necessary for such communication to take place is some means of expressing extensions of a particular signifier or word. Since Scripture provides such a means for God to express the extensions of his peculiar concepts, the only thing that would prevent God from communicating his concepts to us is a belief on our part that we either come naturally equipped with a knowledge of them, and so have no need for God to communicate them to us, or that God's concepts are so radically different from our own that they are unknowable.

Of course, the communication that occurs through Scripture is not unlike other forms of communication, and, as with other forms of communication, sometimes the intentional meaning of the author is not important. When I am told that the next train for Paris is leaving at a particular time, I do not have to know how the person who is communicating to me conceptualizes time, or her personal concept of Paris. Likewise, some communications from God may require no more depth of understanding than the understanding my dog has of my verbal expression, "roll over." The purpose of Scripture, however, is not limited to such simple communication. Through the Scripture, God also wishes to communicate his personal understanding for the purpose of intimacy. In order to communicate on this deeper level, we need to better understand the personal concepts that are so unique to God alone.

Throughout this text, we will suppose that God's concepts may be radically different than our own, but they are nevertheless knowable. The method by which we come to know even God's most radically different concepts is not unlike the hermeneutic method described by Hans-Georg Gadamer. Gadamer speaks of our prejudices being the very things which allow us to enter the conceptual world which humans have constructed in language. Once we have entered that world by accepting the conceptual prejudices of our culture, however, we often discover that such prejudicial concepts do not well account for what we find there. Based upon those experiences and our inherent freedom of imagination, we are able to form new concepts. These new concepts are now the prejudices we use in order to understand the world of our experience. But again, we find evidence within our further experience that proves that our concepts are still prejudicial and in need of yet additional reform. This is what Gadamer, and Heidegger before him, referred to as the "hermeneutic circle," and such a method of continual reform is certainly applicable to our understanding of Scripture as well (Gadamer 7-17).

Just as our prejudicial concepts allow us to enter the conceptual world of our culture and language community, those prejudices also allow us to enter the world of the biblical text. Of course, once having entered Scripture, if we are aware of the prejudicial and all-too-human nature of our concepts, we begin to notice instances within the text that do not conform to our conceptual prejudice. The thing to do in encountering such instances is to allow them to reform our concepts and thus renew our minds, in the same way that Gadamer suggests we continually reform our prejudicial concepts based upon our experience of the world in general.

These new concepts allow us to interpret the biblical text in new ways, but even with these new reformed concepts, we still encounter instances in Scripture which further reveal the prejudicial nature of our concepts and the need for still more reform. This hermeneutic circle, by which we continually reconstruct our conceptual understanding, is what brings us ever closer to God's intentional meaning.

This process will not always be easy, and the situation is a little more difficult than we have thus far explained. For one thing, many instances which God intends as extensions or examples of a certain concept may not be recognized as such because our prejudice has been toward ever more narrow and precise concepts rather than toward broader and richer ones. This narrowing of our concepts has been an overriding cultural prejudice throughout the Western tradition, and especially modernity, and may prevent us from seeing certain Scriptural instances as within the scope and extension of a particular concept. Because of this, it is often easy to miss much of the richness and fullness that many of God's concepts entail.

Additionally, some of God's concepts cannot be communicated simply by setting forth instances in Scripture which serve as extensions of them. Still others may be difficult to communicate because there simply are no earthly extensions of them. Numerous other factors complicate the situation as well, but in spite of these difficulties, I believe it is possible to reconstruct our concepts in ways that give us ever greater insights into God's intentional meaning, if we are aware of how insufficient our conceptual prejudices are and are willing to allow those prejudices to be reformed by what we find in Scripture.

In the following chapters, our purpose is not only to reconstruct some key concepts but also to give examples of how we might deal with some of the difficulties that stand in the way of reconstruction. These suggestions are just that and are not intended to represent the final word on these matters or be representative of God's ultimate intentional meaning. What we offer here are simply new prejudices, but ones that I believe will prove more fruitful and bring us a little closer to God's intentional meaning than the prejudices presently offered by our culture.

Chapter 3

The Concept of Love and the Role of Metaphor, Analogy, and Parable in a Postmodern Hermeneutics

We all have some concept of love. We initially form our concept of love through a set of instances that are identified by the signifier "love." Many of us had a better set of instances than others and thus formed a different and better concept than those who experienced a set of instances that although labeled "love" were less than ideal. But whatever our concept was, when we come to Scripture, we find instances of love that do not fit with the concept of love that we have acquired from our language community.

John 3:16 presents an instance of love that is unimaginably sacrificial, and, in Luke 23:34, we see the forgiving nature of God's love when Jesus, from the cross, asks that his tormenters be forgiven. But there are many more instances of God's love that further add to the concept he is interested in communicating to us in order that we could better understand his heart and mind.

Many of these additional instances are not as obvious as John 3:16 or Jesus' plea from the cross for the forgiveness of his tormentors. The reason they are not as obvious is that, in addition to our conceptual prejudices which blind us to certain extensions of God's concepts, the instances which would express extensions of God's concept of love are often couched in metaphor, analogy, and parable.

The role of things such as metaphors, analogies, and parables has a distinctly different place and importance in postmodern hermeneutics than it had in the hermeneutics of modernity which was intent upon the Enlightenment quest to reduce our understanding to an exact and objective meaning. Metaphoric language certainly seems contrary to the purposes of modernity, and, although it appears throughout Scripture, under modernity it was relegated to a place of secondary importance. In postmodern hermeneutics, however, the situation is quite different. If we begin with an understanding that we are naturally estranged from God's concepts, and that they may be especially foreign to our own, metaphorical instances presented in analogies and parables are as good a way as any, and maybe even the only way, for God to make his concepts known to us. Since concepts, for the most part, are acquired through their extensions, a concept that is particularly abstract or foreign to us may require instances that are particularly metaphorical. If we are seeking a concept of *horse* that would represent all horses, the concept is easily formed out of concrete instances of horses, but if the concept is particularly abstract, or, as in the case of God's concepts, particularly foreign, there may be no obvious instances to serve as extensions of the concept. Certainly, by Jesus having come into the world, we do have some concrete instances which serve as extensions of God's concept of love, as we see with John 3:16 or Luke 23:34, but even with the fact that Jesus has come, there are aspects of God's love that cannot be instanced simply by pointing to examples from the life of Jesus. It would seem that for those aspects metaphor, analogy, and parable are the best means God has available.

Consider the story of Jonah. After Jonah had preached repentance to Nineveh, he sat outside the city to see what would become of the city.

Then the Lord God provided a vine and made it grow up over Jonah to give shade for his head to ease his discomfort, and Jonah was very happy about the vine. But at dawn the next day God provided a worm, which chewed the vine so that it withered. When the sun rose, God provided a scorching east wind, and the sun blazed on Jonah's head so that he grew faint. He wanted to die, and said, "It would be better for me to die than to live.

But God said to Jonah, "Do you have a right to be angry about the vine?"

"I do," he said. "I am angry enough to die."

But the Lord said, "You have been concerned about this vine, though you did not tend it or make it grow. It sprang up overnight and died overnight But Nineveh has more than a hundred and twenty thousand people who cannot tell their right hand from their left, and many cattle as well. Should I not be concerned about that great city?" (Jon. 4:6-11 NIV)

God says that Jonah was concerned for the vine which he did not tend or make to grow. In fact, Jonah's only concern for the vine was that it brought him pleasure. That seems to be the nature of human affection. We like those things that bring us pleasure, and once the pleasure ceases, the cause of the affection ceases. God's love for Nineveh, by contrast, exists even though its people may not bring him pleasure. They are his creation, and for that, rather than that they gratify some need in him, he loves them. Furthermore, God sees that, if they could be brought to repentance, there would be an ever greater capacity for him to continue his creation within them. What this story adds to the concept of love that God is trying to communicate to us is that unlike humans, whose love is basically a desire to have our needs satisfied, God loves and has a passion for his creation.

Human love amounts to the desire to acquire that which we believe will satisfy our want and desire for pleasure. Such a love produces a selfishness and contempt for others. If you and I desire to acquire the same thing in order to satisfy our desire for pleasure, my pleasure can only be realized at the cost of your pleasure. Thus, what we so often desire is obtained at the expense of others, and other human beings are often seen as obstacles to what we conceive of as our happiness. By contrast, God's desire is not to acquire, for he is in need of nothing. His desire is the ultimate pleasure of creation. John Piper has written extensively on Jonathan Edwards' idea that the end for which God created the world is "his own glory, and that this aim is no other than the endless, ever-increasing joy of his people in that glory" (Piper 32). Thus, since God's glory is the ever greater perfection of his creation, there is no conflict between his happiness and our own. Indeed, God's glory and our perfect happiness are identical.

> God in seeking his glory seeks the good of his creatures, because the emanation of his glory (which he seeks and delights in, as he delights in himself and his own eternal glory) implies the communicated excellency and happiness of his creatures. And in communicating his fullness for them, he does it for himself, because their good, which he seeks, is so much in union and communion with himself. (Edwards, *The End* 176)

The fact that God's love is a desire to impart or create is obvious when we consider that divine affection is the affection of a creator for his creatures. It is even obvious that, as our father, God demonstrates a desire for creation. But God's desire for creation is not limited to his being our Creator and Father; it extends even to include the affection he has for us as our Lover. This can be seen in the analogies and parables of the New Testament.

In the fifth chapter of Ephesians, the analogy that God uses to express an extension of his kind of love toward the church is that of a husband's love toward his wife. There are many aspects to this analogy, but one of the most important is the fact that there is not a reciprocity with the concept of love that is being set forth here. Unlike the concept of love that we have received from our culture in which both parties reciprocate the same affection for each other, the analogy here suggests a different kind of affection on the part of the husband and Christ than that of the wife and church. The affection of the husband and Christ is one which involves a headship (Eph. 5:23), a sacrifice (Eph. 5:25), and a nourishing and cherishing (Eph. 5:29) that is not reciprocated by the wife or church. Our love toward Christ does not involve any initiation or headship on our part, and neither is it sacrificial the way his love is toward us. Equally, we do not respond by nourishing and cherishing him as he nourishes and cherishes us. Our love toward him is rather a response of reverence and awe (Eph. 5:33).

But perhaps the most striking way that God's love toward us is different than our love toward him is seen in another aspect of the husband/wife analogy. Since God's love involves a desire to impart life to us, it parallels the husband's desire to impart life to his wife by impregnating her. As strange as this may sound, it does seem that God's love for us involves his desire that we would be impregnated with his seed in order to bring forth new life. This idea may be repugnant to some, but I believe it is biblical and can be seen throughout the New Testament. It is especially evident in the seed parables. There are thirty-seven references to seed in the New Testament. They are all metaphorical and contained within several parables. In Matthew 13:3-43, we are presented with three parables in which God sows seed in order to produce life. The second of these three is the parable about the tares.

> The kingdom of heaven is likened unto a man which sowed good seed in his field; But while men slept, his enemy came and sowed tares among his wheat . . . (Matt 13:24-25 KJV)

Later, when his disciples ask him to explain the parable, Jesus says,

> He that soweth the good seed is the Son of man; the field is the world; the good seed are the children of the kingdom; but the tares are the children of the wicked one; The enemy that sowed them is the devil . . . (Matt. 13:37-39 KJV)

Here we are told that the sower of the seed is the Son of man. Indeed, Jesus is one who impregnates and plants his seed within us, in order that new life might come forth. It is his seed that causes the new birth and makes us into the children of God.

In the Gospel of Luke, only the first of the parables that Matthew offered is presented: the parable of the seed that falls on different ground.

A sower went out to sow his seed: and as he sowed, some fell by the way side; and it was trodden down, and the fowls of the air devoured it. Some fell upon a rock; and as soon as it was sprung up, it withered away because it lacked moisture. And some fell among thorns; and the thorns sprang up with it, and choked it. And other fell on good ground, and sprang up, and bare fruit an hundredfold. (Luke 8:5-8 KJV)

In explaining this parable, Jesus says, "Now the parable is this: The seed is the word of God" (Luke 8:11 KJV). This parable seems to be different from the parable of the tares, in that with the parable of the tares the seed were the children of the kingdom. But is the seed analogy different in these two parables, or is the word of God the very seed that produces the children of the kingdom?

Just as my physical existence began as a seed, in the same way my life in Christ began as a seed – namely, the word of God. Indeed, my life in Christ began when I opened myself and allowed the word of God to impregnate me.

Being born again, not of corruptible seed, but of incorruptible, by the word of God, which liveth and abideth forever. (1 Peter 1:23 KJV)

How exactly this happens, we do not know (Mark 4:26-27). It is indeed a mystery, but as mysterious as this process is, the analogy is quite clear: God's love for us involves a desire that we would open ourselves and allow Jesus' words to impregnate us and bring forth life.

This understanding that God's love is a desire and passion for creation, and that the means that God employs to bring about that creation are words, is also tied to the biblical concept of prophecy. For most of us, our cultural understanding is that prophecy is a form of fortune telling or predicting the future, and indeed there are places where that does seem to be the meaning Scripture intends. At other times, however, the instances of prophecy seem to connote the broader concept of speaking for God, or making a divinely inspired utterance. It is this broader sense that Jesus must intend when he says, "For all the prophets and the law prophesied until John"

(Matt. 11:13 KJV). If "the law prophesied," we cannot understand "prophesied" as having predicted the future. We can, however, understand the law as speaking for God or representing a divinely inspirited communication. Of course, God's words often do precede some future state of affairs, but it is not that they predict the future but rather that they create it. Words in general are often creative even when they are of human rather than divine origin. The things we tell our children about themselves come to pass, not because we are all-knowing seers but because words have power. When words are spoken by God, or someone who speaks for God, they are especially powerful and have the ability to create or destroy.

Now some biblical instances of prophetic utterances create blessing or doom independent of any participation on the part of the people for whom the words are intended. In other instances, however, some participation on the part of the person for whom the words are intended is necessary. For example, Christians believe that everything Jesus said was a prophetic utterance, and much of what he said was intended to bless those to whom he spoke. In many of those instances, however, it was necessary that the persons to whom Jesus spoke received his words. This is not because they were not as powerful as those utterances that create a reality independent of the person to whom they are addressed, but because they are the words of a lover rather than a creator or father. As creator, God spoke the universe into existence, and there was no participation on our part. As my personal creator, God required no participation on my part as well. Equally, the words of a father do not require the consent of the child. But words of a lover do require the consent of the beloved. Indeed, the beloved must choose to open herself to the lovers words and allow those words to have their effect. As God's creatures or children, we had no choice but to accept his creative love, but as his beloved, we do have a choice. We must choose to become his beloved and receive his seed. If we are to be made into the fullness of his image and bring forth new life, we must first be impregnated and that requires a consent on our part. Those who have not been impregnated by the word of God that Jesus brings may look like Christians, they may even act like Christians and do miracles in Jesus' name, but if they were never impregnated by him, he never knew them, and they are not his beloved.

> Many will say to me in that day, Lord, Lord, have we not prophesied in thy name? and in thy name have case out devils? and in thy name done many wonderful works? And then will I profess unto them, I never knew you: depart from me. . . . (Matt. 7:22-23 KJV)

It is difficult to interpret this passage, and in particular the word *knew*, in any other way but as a personal intimacy, as when Scripture says, "Adam knew Eve his wife; and she conceived" (Gen. 4:1 KJV). To understand the word in any other way simply does not make sense. God knows all things. The hairs of our head are all counted, so no one escapes his notice, but many refuse the kind of intimacy that would allow his seed to produce life within them. He may be their Creator, but they have never become his beloved because they have never given themselves over to be impregnated by him. As their creator, he gave them life (over which they had no choice), but, concerning the new life that he wants to give them, they do have a choice. In order to have that new life, they must surrender themselves and allow him to become their lover by impregnating them with his seed. In this case, they do have a choice and indeed they must choose to whom they are to be joined.

> Or do you not know that the one who joins himself to a harlot is one body with her? For he says, "the two will become one flesh." But the one who joins himself to the Lord is one spirit with him. (1 Cor. 6:16-17 KJV)

With all these metaphorical analogies and parables it appears that the intimacy which the Scripture tells us God desires is nothing less than the intimate union that produces new life. In this intimate union, God is the lover and giver of life, and we are the beloved who receive that life.

Again, with this notion of love that is being set forth by the biblical instances there is no reciprocity as there is with our contemporary, cultural notions of love. We cannot impregnate Christ or give our seed to him as he gives his seed to us. A consequence of this is that we can never be God's lover, and we can never have toward him the same kind of divine love he has toward us. Toward God we will always be the beloved, having a human love that desires to acquire rather than to impart. This may seem strange since we are called to be like him, and especially to have his kind of love. How then are we to do that? It must be that, in order to take on the divine nature and become divine lovers, we must do so toward other human beings and not toward God. Although we cannot be God's lover with anything but a human, acquisitive love, we can be the lovers of other human beings and have for them the same divine love God has for us. Indeed, we can impregnate others with the same words of life that we have been impregnated with.

Consequently, the idea that we can be Christians and take on the nature of Jesus, and the nature of his love, simply through our relationship with him is wrong. It may seem that the Christian life can be lived, and can be lived best, when one is in constant and exclusive communion with God. But God's purpose for our lives can never be realized in that way. If we are to take on God's nature, and if divine love is to exist within us, others besides God and ourselves are required in order that we may be the lover and impart to them the same words of life that God has imparted to us.

By conceptualizing divine love as a desire or passion to create and impart, and therefore distinctly different from human love which is acquisitive, we also have a better insight into certain key Scriptures concerning love. This is particularly true of 1Corinthians 13. Commentaries abound on this Scripture, but with our understanding that God's concept of love is not a desire to acquire but a passion to create, we have a better basis for interpreting this chapter, especially verses four to eight, in which a series of statements are made concerning what love is and what love is not. Another way to understand these characteristics is to see the positive characteristics as aspects of God's divine love, while the characteristics that are presented negatively are aspects of human love. In fact, that would seem to be the only sensible way to interpret the difference between what love is and what it is not, since an enormous list could be given concerning what love is not. Love is not an apple or a planet, a color, or an insect. The list could go on forever. The only way a list of things which love is not would be meaningful is if that list consisted of things which are in fact not characteristics of love, though they are commonly thought to be characteristics of love. That is, they are what human beings often conceive to be characteristic of love, but they are not part of God's concept of love.

Consider the characteristics that are presented in the negative. Love is

> not jealous, love does not brag and is not arrogant, does not act unbecomingly; it does not seek its own, is not provoked, does not take into account a wrong suffered, does not rejoice in unrighteousness . . . (1 Cor. 13:4b-6a NAS)

Although we are told that these characteristics are not what love is, they do appear to be characteristic of what we often conceive love to be. That is, human, acquisitive love certainly is jealous. In fact, love, as humans so often conceive it, is what most often causes jealousy because what I desire to acquire may also be desired by another. Likewise, human, acquisitive love is braggadocios and arrogant when it succeeds in acquiring the things it desires. The person who loves fame or money boasts when her love has conquered and attained its object. Equally, the very thing that causes people to act most unbecoming is the driving lust to acquire what they love and what they believe will satisfy their desires. Acquisitive love certainly does seek its own. Human, acquisitive love is essentially the desire to possess. It also often provokes us to do things that we would otherwise find unimaginable. Indeed, it is often the very thing which causes us to act unbecomingly. Likewise, a wrong suffered is intensified and made all the more difficult to bear when it involves love – at least love as humans so often conceive it. And certainly a lover scorned rejoices in the unrighteousness of revenge, which should be reserved for God alone. These characteristics presented in the negative certainly are characteristics of love, at least as it is so often conceptualized by human beings.

By contrast, the positive characteristics seem indicative of the kind of divine love which desires to impart and create within the beloved rather than to acquire unto itself.

> Love is patient, love is kind . . . (love) rejoices with the truth; bears all things, believes all things, hopes all things, endures all things. Love never fails. (1 Cor. 13:4a-8a NAS)

Patience is certainly a characteristic of creation. In fact, our experience tells us that the more perfect the creation, the more patience is required. Kindness – or as it is often translated, gentleness – is another requisite of creation. The more perfect the creation, the more concerned and gentle the act of creation needs to be. Additionally, the creation of a perfection within the beloved certainly involves an enduring and bearing all things. It especially must endure and bear the rejection that the lover so often suffers at the hand of the beloved. Furthermore, essential to divine love or the love of creation is the ability to hope and believe. Without hope and belief, that which is not can never come to be. Indeed, the truth in which creative, divine love rejoices is not the truth of what is, but the truth of what is to be. It is a truth not found in the circumstances of this world, but a truth found in the hope and beliefs of the creator. This is the truth in which God rejoices.

In concluding this chapter, we should mention again that what is being set forth here is not a comprehensive and definitive understanding of love. This treatment is certainly not exhaustive, and we may find other aspects of God's love which are communicated through the biblical instances which add still further to the personal concept of love which God is trying to communicate. Our intention is rather to be suggestive and offer examples of how we could discover, in Scripture, extensions of a concept like love which might give us additional insights into God's intentional meaning.

Chapter 4

Broadening, Enriching, and Debunking the Concept of Love

As mentioned earlier, one thing that makes this process of reconstructing our concepts according to biblical instances difficult is that we have a certain confidence that our cultural concepts are sufficient and not in need of reform. Because of this confidence in our all-too-human concepts, we are prevented from recognizing certain biblical instances as extensions of a particular concept that God is trying to communicate. The concept of God's love, especially the sacrificial nature of that love, is a good example of a concept that is not fully communicated because we come to Scriptures with a confidence that we already have a sufficient notion of what a loving sacrifice should look like. This confidence in our own concepts prevents us from recognizing certain biblical instances that might stretch our understanding and provide us a better idea of God's intentional meaning.

Of course, Scripture does set forth several instances that do attest to the sacrificial nature of God's love. John 3:16 says that God's love for the world caused him to give his only begotten Son, and John 15:13 tells us that "greater love has no one than this, that one lay down his life for his friends." Furthermore, Scripture also states that Christ "laid down his life for us" (1 John 3:16 KJV), and husbands are told that they are to love their wives "even as Christ also loved the church and gave himself for it" (Eph. 5:25 KJV). In spite of these scriptural instances, however, God's concept remains at least partially foreign to us, and the sacrificial nature of God's love is not fully communicated because we believe we have enough of a concept to represent God's intentional meaning. Such a confidence prevents us from recognizing other instances which might broaden our concept of God's sacrificial love. Indeed, if God wished to stretch our concept of a loving sacrifice by giving us instances which feel outside the scope or extension of our concept, would we be able to recognize them as instances of a loving sacrifice? If we believe that our concepts are adequate and reflect God's intentional meaning, we are only able to recognize instances which are extensions of our existing concept. As a result, even if God were to set forth in Scripture instances in order to communicate the full extent of his concept of love, we may not recognize such instances since they extend beyond the scope or extension of our concept.

If I have a concept of *dog*, I will be able to pick out instances or examples of dogs as these instances fall within the scope or extension of my concept. If, on the other hand, someone else has a different concept of *dog* which includes particular animals that are not included in the extension of my concept, I would be wrong to believe that I understood her concept simply because we both used the same word, *dog*. I could, however, acquire her concept if I first understood that it was foreign to me and then began looking for instances of her concept that were not included in the extension of my own concept.

This is certainly the case with God's communication to human beings. In order to communicate his foreign concepts to us, he gives us instances in Scripture which go beyond the extension of our concepts. Unfortunately, since we so often come to

Scripture with the prejudice that we have adequate concepts, we often miss those instances which might renew our minds and bring us into a better understanding of God's intentional meaning.

One such instance is presented in Judges 19, which involves a story of a man whose concubine runs away and returns to her father's house. The man pursues her and convinces her to return with him. At the end of the first day of the journey, they must stay overnight in Gibeah, a city of Benjamin. They initially camp in the town square, but they meet an old man who invites them to stay with him. They accept his hospitality, but during the course of the evening, some rowdies from the town come and demand that the old man give them the stranger that is staying in his house in order that they might sodomize him. The old man begs the rowdies to spare the stranger and instead offers his own virgin daughter that they might ravage her rather than the stranger.

I often ask students what kind of father the old man was. Would you vote for him for father-of-the-year? Would you want such a man as your own father? How do you explain such behavior? Some point to this as an example of sexism in the Old Testament, but it is hard to imagine how sexist beliefs would cause someone to voluntarily give his own daughter in order to save a stranger merely because he was a man and she was a woman. It is much more likely that this story is instead set forth as an instance of God's love. Indeed, as strange as this old man's behavior seems, it is exactly what the Christian God does. When I was still a stranger, God was saying to those who wished to ravage and destroy me, "Take my son instead. He is a virgin: ravage and kill him, but spare this stranger." This story seems to serve a similar function to the parables of the New Testament, in which God tries to communicate his conceptual meaning to us by setting forth instances which serve as extensions of a particular concept he is attempting to communicate.

In discussing this story with students, I often ask what would be their price for agreeing to give their child over to be tortured and killed. Humans always have a price. For what price would you turn your child over to be tortured and killed?

Would you do it for billions of dollars, fame, eternal beauty? What would be your price? I always receive the same unanimous answer. As corrupt as human beings are, they would never do such a thing for any price. But Scripture tells us that God did have a price. Indeed, a world of lost sinners was the price which he accepted in exchange for his son. A line from the hymn "How Great Thou Art" says,

> And when I think that God, his Son not sparing, sent him to die, I scarce can take it in.

But the truth is not that we scarcely take it in – the truth is that we cannot take it in. It is truly beyond our imagination, but this story in Judges does at least give us a glimpse of God's love and how its sacrificial nature goes beyond anything we can imagine.

Of course, the story in Judges and the story of the gospel are not perfectly analogical. In the story from Judges, the old man does not give his virgin daughter, but instead the concubine is substituted and given to be ravaged and killed (of course, this is the Old Testament where the sacrificial lamb is substituted for the ultimate sacrifice of God's own son). Furthermore, in the gospel story, Jesus freely agrees, and God does not sacrifice his virgin son against his will. There is no mention in Judges that the virgin daughter approves of her father's suggestion. In light of the fact that it is not a perfect analogy, some might think it is stretching the Scripture to see this episode as an example or instance of the sacrificial nature of God's love. Of course, we are not actually stretching the Scripture at all. What we are stretching, however, is our imagination, and we are doing so, not to create new doctrines based on more exact and narrow notions of what the Scripture means, but rather to broaden our notions of some of God's most important concepts. Such stretching is exactly what is needed if we are to come to better understand God's concepts and so obtain a richer sense of his intentional meaning.

Modernity has led us to believe that what is needed are ever more exact and precise concepts, after the model of mathematics, but if we wish to come to understand another person's personal concepts, we generally need to move in the opposite direction toward broader concepts rather than narrower ones. The science of modernity also led us to believe that our goal should be to eliminate the imagination and thus gain an objective understanding, but, if we are to understand the personal concepts of another individual, the imagination is necessary. Indeed, in trying to come to grips with the personal concepts of another person, I am constantly trying to imagine what he has in mind. Instead of passively listening as he sets forth instances that might serve as extensions of his concept, I actively try to imagine his concept and may even suggest instances on my own and ask if such instances fall within the extension of the concept he is trying to communicate.

The same can be done with the concepts that God is trying to communicate to us. Not that we can query God directly concerning whether this or that instance falls within the scope of his concept, but we can bring to the biblical text instances that have their origin far afield of Scripture to see if such instances are indeed consistent with the concept that the scriptural instances create. By doing so, we overcome the narrowness of our cultural concepts and broaden our understanding in order to reflect the richness of God's concepts.

As an example, consider the claim of Jose Ortega y Gasset that "attention" is an essential aspect of love. He claims that within the consciousness of the lover there is the constant presence of the beloved. He says,

> Falling in love, initially, is no more than this: attention abnormally fastened upon another person. (Ortega y Gasset 64)

This certainly seems true of the love that exists between people who are "in love." Indeed, lovers are individuals who have their attention abnormally fixed upon their beloveds. "For the lover his beloved . . . possesses a constant presence" (Ortega y Gasset 65), and occupies the lover's attention in a way that nothing else can.

Of course, when Ortega y Gasset says that "'falling in love' is a phenomenon of attention" (62), he is referring specifically to the relationship between a man and a woman, or the idea of romantic love, but what he describes is also descriptive of other forms of love, and it is what we all desire in terms of being loved. The affection children desire from their parents largely involves attention, in the same way that the affection we desire in a romantic relationship largely involves attention. Even friendships, if they are to be meaningful, require that we are capable of fixing our attention upon our friend, and if someone we consider a friend is unwilling to give us her attention, we feel we may have been mistaken in considering her a friend in the first place.

Unfortunately, however, as much as we desire the attention of spouses, parents, or friends, we human beings are not very good at fixing our attention on any one thing for very long periods of time. Ortega y Gasset points out that the attention of a normal human being is constantly changing from one object to another (62-63). Because of this, we are a constant disappointment to our spouses, children, and friends. My wife's disappointment in me, as a lover, usually focuses on my lack of attention. "You're not here" being her complaint. And although I try to assure her that I was listening and can even repeat what she said, her complaint is still valid. I may have been listening, but I wasn't attentive. My wife knows that to be truly loved is a matter of attention, and she is frustrated by my lack of attention. Small children seem instinctively to know the same thing and evidence it by clamoring to their mothers, "watch me!"

Of course, parents disappoint children, just as husbands disappoint wives, because human attention is fleeting even concerning the things we love most. Indeed, if a lover is one who fixes his attention on his beloved, then the vast majority of human beings make poor lovers. Fortunately, our desire to be loved by one who gives us extraordinary attention is not completely frustrated, "and there is a friend that sticketh closer than a brother" (Prov. 18:24 KJV). Fortunately, God's omnipresent and omniscient nature makes him quite different from human beings in this regard. He is capable of giving us attention in ways that other human beings are not. Unlike other human beings who constantly fail us in this regard, God says, "My eyes and my heart will always be there" (2 Chr. 7:16 NIV). Indeed, his "eyes will be open" and his "ears attentive" (2 Chr. 7:15 NIV), and "like an eagle that stirs up its nest and hovers over its young" (Deut. 32:10-11 NIV), he will attend to us as "the apple of his eye" (Zech. 2:8 NIV).

It is his omnipresent and omniscient nature that makes God the supreme lover and the only one who can truly satisfy our desire for attention. Of course, the attention he gives us is not mechanical and the result merely of his omniscient and omnipresent nature. It is rather the result of his will. His nature makes him aware of the whole of his creation, but he has chosen to make us into the image of his son and the centerpiece of that creation.

It is also interesting that attention is an attribute of both divine and human love and, although existing in an imperfect degree in human beings, our love for God is largely a matter of attention just as his love toward us is largely a matter of attention. Thus, unlike the desire to impregnate and bring forth offspring in the beloved, attention is a characteristic of divine love that is reciprocal. Indeed, we love God to the extent that God is in all our thoughts. Just as children measure the love of their parents by the amount and quality of the attention they give them, and wives measure the love of their husbands by their attention, we can measure our love toward God by attention as well. Furthermore, it is good that we consider the measure of our attention toward God. For when we see how minuscule our attention is in comparison to his worthiness, and likewise, how perfect his attention is in spite of our unworthiness, we should be humbled and brought to a correct perspective of God and ourselves.

Attention then should be a major attribute that goes into the concept of love that God is trying to communicate to us. And although neither the Bible nor our mainstream culture explicitly points to attention as a central ingredient in love, when put to the biblical test, it does appear to be part of the concept God would want to communicate to us.

While attention appears to pass the biblical test, however, other characteristics do not. Such characteristics, however, can be debunked by the same simple method. One such example is the idea that an ever-growing passion and an excitement are essential to true love. Although commonly thought to be an attribute of love in its most ideal form, when put to the biblical test, an increasing passion and excitement are not descriptive of, or essential to, the concept of love that is set forth in Scripture.

To begin with, it certainly is not the nature of God's divine love to increasingly burn with passion and excitement for what he desires. God's love, being a desire to impart or create rather than acquire, is not a desire that grows in intensity and fervor. As we have seen, the creative passion requires things such as patience and gentleness which are incompatible with an increased intensity of desire and excitement.

Of course, as we have argued, it could be that we are to have a different kind of love toward him than he has toward us. As we have seen, our love toward God is acquisitive and therefore different than his love toward us. But even that acquisitive love, which is so different from God's love, does not involve an ever-increasing passion, as is often imagined.

This is not to say that we are not to desire God, but rather that the degree of intense excitement that accompanies our desire is a poor measure of our love for God. In fact, desire in itself, even when it is directed toward God, is never a good thing. Only the end to which it points is good. Desire is certainly useful in that it points to a good, but desire in itself is not a virtue, but a sign of lack and want.

Scripture does speak of men seeking after God's own heart (Acts 13:22), but the value of that desire is found in the fact that it is "after God" and not that it is an especially intense desire on the part of that individual. There are no Scriptures to indicate that there is something good, noble, or worthy in the quantity or quality of our desire.

A thirst after God is certainly good, but only because it brings us to God and not because thirst in itself is good. It is good that the deer pants after the water brook (Ps. 42:1), lest it die of thirst. But it would not be good for the deer to be in a constant state of panting. In fact, the ideal would be to have water which could be drunk in order that we would thirst no more. This is the water that Jesus gives (John 4:10-15).

Of course, we are to desire to be ever more obedient, more attentive, more cooperative, and more understanding of God ways, but to desire to be more desirous is not a virtue and does not bring us any closer to God. It is a common but serious mistake to think that the more intense our desire is, the more pleasing it is to God. That may be true of the kind of love and glory that human beings seek. Indeed, we may desire to be loved by others who burn with passion for us, but God has no such want, and to think that he does is to believe that our all-too-human concept of love and glory is identical to his concept. To believe that God is gratified in proportion to the intensity of our passion for him is wrongly to believe that the fervor and excitement behind our desire satisfy a want in him.

Surely God is pleased with our desire for him. His pleasure, however, comes from the fact that he loves his creation, and he wants that creation to come into the perfection he has for it. Such perfection requires that we desire him and are open to the perfection he wishes to create within us. The idea that we are to love God with all of our heart, soul, and mind (Matt. 22:37) should be taken to mean that we are open to God and his perfecting love in all of the areas of our lives. Even in Deuteronomy 6:5 which substitutes "strength" where Matthew 22:37 says "mind," the word "strength" should not be understood as an ennobling passion. Indeed, to understand the desire we are to have for God as increasing in value as it increases in intensity is to misconceive the nature of his love and glory as acquisitive rather than creative. It is to conceive of God's glory from a perspective that is all-too-human.

The idea that God is gratified by the intensity of our passion for him, however, is not founded simply in the fact that we conceive love and glory in an acquisitive, human way and then naively assume that God's concept is no different from our own.

It is also, in many cases, the result of a pride in our religious zeal that brings us to believe that such a lustful passion wins us favor with God.

Of course, some people's temperaments may be such that their reaction to God, and what he is doing in their lives, is extremely emotional and zealous. There is certainly nothing wrong with this, but it is mistaken to think that the intensity of that zeal produces spiritual fruit and should be the model for all to follow. Spiritual growth and maturity is not connected to a growth in the intensity of our desire but a growth in our submission to God and an increased sensitivity to, and understanding of, his will. To believe that our desire gains worth with its intensity is detrimental to the Christian life. It produces frustration and discouragement when we come to think that our love is not as intense as it should be, and pride when we are deceived into thinking that it is of superior intensity.

It is a similar misconception to believe that our love for God should include a desire for ever more spectacular manifestations of God's presence. Of course, the Christian life certainly is about experiencing God's presence. It may begin as a belief in the historical death and resurrection of Jesus, but that belief is intended to bring us into an ongoing experience with the risen Christ who so graciously brings us into the peace and sweetness of his father's presence. The writers of Psalms, as well as later Christian writers such as Brother Lawrence (Practicing the Presence of God) and Madame Guyon (Experiencing the Depths of Jesus Christ) tell us of how accessible God is and how much he desires that we would dwell in his omnipresence. We are deceived, however, when we come to believe that the experiencing of the omnipresence of God is not of equal value to our experience of a more spectacular manifestation of God's presence. Such spectacular manifestations of God's presence may be part of the Christian life, but they contain no more peace or sweetness than those times when we experience the omnipresence of God which he has made so accessible to us through the sacrifice of his son. It is God and his presence that we are after and not the form of the manifestation. Thus, it is mistake to believe that we are to desire such spectacular experiences and value them as somehow superior to other experiences of God's presence.

Fortunately such wrong concepts of love can be debunked by the same method that we used to discover that "attention" was a genuine attribute of love. And so, with the same simple method of bringing to Scripture the concepts which represent the cultural and historical prejudices that make up our understanding, we can test our concepts against what we find in Scripture. By so doing, we reform our concepts and renew our minds, and so make them a little richer, fuller, and less amiss of God's intentional meaning.

Chapter 5

The Concept of Forgiveness

Some concepts are difficult to communicate because there are no instances within our experience to which God might point as extensions of his own concept. Even in these cases, however, we are often able to come to an understanding of how immeasurably far his concept exceeds our own. Of course, such an understanding is only possible if we realize the all-too-human nature of our concepts and come to reflect upon what is given in Scripture with a desire to have our minds renewed in a way that would bring us ever closer to God's intentional meaning. Forgiveness serves as an example of such a concept.

The idea of forgiveness that we acquired from our language community and culture is certainly different than God's concept of forgiveness, but as different as it is, it seems more to be a difference of degree than of kind. Forgiveness, in both cases, is that by which one releases from any guilt another who has caused them harm, in order that the relationship between those individuals might be restored. The extent to which this ever takes place among human beings is so meager that the concept we form from human examples can hardly be taken as extensions which might communicate God's concept. The cliche "to err is human, to forgive divine" may not be a cliche at all but a deep truism. Human beings find forgiveness extremely difficult, and because there are so few instances of it, it is not only something we cannot do but it is also something difficult to conceptualize. The extremes of human forgiveness only extend to those rare cases in which individuals are able to "forgive" someone for murdering or torturing a loved one. Such instances of forgiveness, however, merely serve to establish a relationship of distant civility with the guilty. There are no instances of forgiveness in which someone forgave the murder of a loved one and then entered into a loving marriage with that individual. That is the kind of instance that would be needed to communicate God's concept. Since such examples are rare or nonexistent in our experience, the concept we develop of forgiveness is something far less than God's concept. Still, as impossible as it may be for humans to actualize or even conceptualize forgiveness, we can, through reflection, come to understand some of the things that limit our forgiveness and make it something less than God's forgiveness.

One of the things that keeps us from knowing forgiveness as God understands it is our human idea of justice. Justice, at least as human beings commonly understand it, is the idea that the guilty should be made to pay for any harm they have done. We are told in Scripture to be just and thus be willing, when we are guilty of harming others, to pay for the harm we have done. While such an idea may be of considerable social utility given the present state of human beings, and may even be a means to restore relationships in cases in which the harm we have done is not too serious and the guilty party is able to compensate the innocent party for what they have done, it is an idea which for the most part is an obstacle to forgiveness. Indeed, a desire for justice when we conceive ourselves as the innocent or offended party is disastrous to relationships, and it is what prevents relationships, once damaged, from being restored.

In addressing the specific relationship of marriage in his book *Men and Women: Enjoying the Difference*, Larry Crabb describes the problem of justice. Crabb points to self-centeredness as the real problem in marriage, but it is not just self-centeredness that is the problem. More specifically, it is "justified self-centeredness," or selfishness clouded with ideas of fairness and justice.

> Careful inspection of ourselves, particularly when we're angry, makes it clear that we suffer from a defect more severe than mere self-centeredness. The greatest obstacle to buidling truly good relationships is *justified* self-centeredness, a selfness that, deep in our souls, feels entirely reasonable and therefore acceptable in light of how we've been treated. (Crabb 65)

From this idea of what is just or fair, husbands reason that they will respond lovingly toward their wives, only if their wives act in a certain way toward them. If wives treat husbands poorly, it would be wrong or unjust for husbands to treat them with love. Husbands reason that they should act justly and behave toward their wives as their wives behave toward them. Such behavior is certainly just and husbands reason that it is the best way to teach their wives that, if they wish to be treated lovingly, they need to behave in a certain way. But although there may be a place for justice given the fallen nature of our world, and it may even be virtuous to seek justice and make payment for our offenses when we are guilty, a desire to seek payment from others in order to establish justice in our relationships is disastrous.

A desire for justice certainly destroys any chance of a relationship becoming truly intimate. That is because an increase in intimacy brings an increase in vulnerability. The more intimate we become with someone, the more the offenses of that person hurt us. An offense that would go unnoticed by a stranger or acquaintance is devastating when leveled by a loved one. Any negative feelings or thoughts that someone has toward us are made more painful if that person is someone with whom we are intimate. Since we are more sensitive to the offenses of loved ones, we are hurt by them with greater frequency than by acquaintances. If we seek justice and demand that the guilty pay for every offense we experience in our intimate unions, those relationships are doomed.

If intimate relationships are to survive, forgiveness is essential. The reason forgiveness is so essential is because it is not merely the opposite of justice but, in another sense, it is the fulfillment of justice. Forgiveness is the opposite of justice in that the innocent, rather than the guilty, pays for the harm that has been done, but it is the fulfillment of justice in that with forgiveness the offense is paid for. When one person does harm to another, the relationship between the two is damaged or destroyed. Someone must pay for that destruction. There is an option, however, concerning which one will suffer for the offense. It could be, as in the case of justice, that the guilty pay for the harm they have done to the innocent and to the relationship. In some cases, justice may bring restoration to the relationship. The other option is for the innocent, who have suffered the harm, to be willing to absorb the hurt and not demand retribution. The harm the innocent willingly suffers is able to restore the relationship in so far as the hurts and harm to the relationship come to an end with the innocents' willingness to pay for the offense of the guilty. The guilty are then able to enjoy the relationship because payment has been made on their behalf by the innocent.

As an example, imagine someone taking a friend's credit card without permission and using it to go on a great vacation. In realizing that the thousands of dollars he has charged to his friend's account has hurt his friend and damaged the relationship he had with him, he desires to restore the relationship. The relationship might be restored through justice, whereby the guilty party compensates his innocent friend for what he has charged to his account. If he is unable to compensate his friend and pay back the money, but still desires that the relationship be restored, forgiveness is the only other option. In restoring the relationship through forgiveness rather than justice, the innocent must be willing to pay for what has been charged to his account and no longer treat his friend as guilty.

Or consider the example of adultery. The one who is hurt is innocent, but if that person truly forgives, he is saying that he is willing to endure that hurt without requiring retribution or some type of payment on the part of the guilty. The injured take on all of the hurt and treat the guilty as if no wrong had been done. The relationship is restored, and the guilty are able to enjoy that relationship as if nothing ever happened. Of course, something did happen, but the innocent one is willing to pay for it, for the sake of restoring the relationship. In fact, the relationship may be even better, at least to the extent that the guilty party realizes that the innocent cherished the relationship to the extent that he is willing to pay dearly to preserve it.

In both cases, the solution of forgiveness remains unappealing to us. It is unfair that the guilty are free from the consequences of what they did and can enjoy their relationship with the innocent as if the offense never took place, while the innocent must suffer the pain of that offense. No one likes pain, but the fact that it is the result of injustice makes it especially difficult to accept. The fact that we find injustice so hard to bear seems to follow from the fact that we generally conceive of ourselves as innocents and imagine that we would never do such a thing to a friend or lover. We readily imagine the injustice being done to us. If we imagined ourselves as the guilty party, we would not find such injustice so unappealing.

Another factor which makes forgiveness rare among human beings is the fact that in order to choose to take the harm upon ourselves, we must value our relationship with that other person as of greater value or importance than our own pain. If we choose to forgive, we may suffer, but the relationship will be saved. Thus, the motivation behind forgiveness is not my own self-interest but the interest of the relationship. Unfortunately, few if any of us love a relationship with someone who has hurt us enough to be willing to suffer much pain in the interest of restoring and preserving that relationship.

For these reasons, we seldom see extensions or examples of true forgiveness in this world, and therefore the concept we form is always less than true forgiveness. Even when people profess to forgive, it is almost always less than what is needed to truly restore a relationship. People who profess to forgive almost always have some way of letting the guilty know that the relationship could be better than it is if not for that unmentionable offense which, though "forgiven," still hampers the relationship. With such imperfect forgiveness, the innocent may wish to preserve the relationship, but they are not willing to take the hurt completely upon themselves but wish to share that pain in some way with the guilty.

But although our idea of justice, our distaste for pain, and our love of ourselves more than our relationships with others eliminate the possibility of examples of God's forgiveness within the human realm, we do have examples set forth in Scripture which serve as extensions of a more divine concept. Certainly Christ from the cross forgiving his tormentors is one such instance. Another is the example of Hosea, who marries a prostitute, only to have her leave him and return to prostitution. Hosea responds with forgiveness, and restores the relationship, after which she leaves him again for a life of prostitution. Hosea goes far beyond what most of us can imagine by restoring her yet again a second time. But as much as such instances go far beyond the human realm of forgiveness, they are meager and do not really serve as an extension capable of communicating God's forgiveness. Such examples are not sufficient to serve as true extensions of God's concept of forgiveness because God's nature is considerably different from our own.

We think it a sign of great piety to be able to forgive the single transgression of a friend or spouse and thus restore a relationship. But what if we were omniscient and we knew of every hateful or unkind thought that a friend or spouse had toward us? If we were aware of every time they thought ill of us, or desired someone else's company rather than ours, none of our relationships would survive. If we were such creatures, we would have no lasting relationships, for none of us have anything near that capacity for forgiveness.

By contrast, God is omniscient and knows every wayward thought we have ever had. He is all wise and knows that when we curse a certain circumstance we find distasteful, we are actually cursing the God who is behind that circumstance. But in spite of being all-knowing and aware of the waywardness that exists in the deepest recesses of our hearts and minds, he forgives us and is willing to suffer that hurt for the sake of the relationship he desires to have with us. Human beings are simply not capable of imagining such forgiveness. We are easily offended, and although we may be able to forgive an offense or two, if we were aware of much more than that, we would have no way of restoring our relationships.

Still, despite our limited capacity and meager understanding, we are called to forgive. Furthermore, there are things we can do to increase our capacity for forgiveness. For one thing, our present meditation does at least bring us to see how meager our concept of forgiveness is in comparison to God's forgiveness. Such an understanding can have a humbling effect upon us, and humility seems to be an essential ingredient if we are to expand our limited natural capacity for forgiveness.

Some people do seem to have a greater capacity for forgiveness, but the reason is not that they have attained a higher spirituality which makes them more godlike - rather, it is quite the opposite. The most forgiving people are the most humble people. They realize, more than others, how poor in spirit they truly are. They decrease and become less concerned with themselves. As they do, the divine quality of forgiveness, which amounts to their willingness to pay for the offenses of those who have harmed them, increases within them. In the light of their own poverty, they are better able to see the greatness of God's forgiveness; in the light of God's forgiveness, they are made more forgiving.

By contrast, proud, self-absorbed people tend to be more limited in their capacity for forgiveness. Proud people with big egos demand justice even over the most minor offenses. To them, any offense is a capital offense because it is against *them*.

Additionally, a correct perspective of other human beings can also aid us in our attempt to expand our ability to forgive. That correct perspective involves understanding man's fallen nature: we are a sinful race whose only hope lies in the greatness of God's forgiveness. From this perspective, we are not shocked or disappointed when others hurt us. We rather anticipate it and equally anticipate our need to forgive.

As we have seen, our impulse toward justice is deeply ingrained because we conceive of ourselves as innocent. Justice is only attractive to the innocent. The guilty never clamor for justice but for forgiveness and mercy. We believe the lie that we are innocents, and we are therefore attracted to the idea of justice. By contrast, as we see the truth of our own guilt, we come to love mercy and become more willing and able to extend forgiveness to others.

Chapter 6

The Concept of Faith

In addition to concepts like love and forgiveness, another important concept in need of reform or reconstruction is faith. In attempting such a reconstruction after the biblical instances, we encounter yet another problem. Thus far, our reconstruction of concepts has been quite simple and has merely treated individual concepts which needed to be broadened and modified to reflect God's intentional meaning. With the concept of faith, however, we need to make some changes to the way we think about concepts in general.

Of course, faith, like love, is also a concept that needs to be broadened because it suffers from a Western tradition that attempts to make our concepts ever more narrow and precise in the name of science. In the Modern period, the quest to conceptualize the world correctly was especially equated with conceptualizing things clearly, and certainly nothing could be more clear than to have concepts of the kind we find in mathematics. Unfortunately, personal concepts are quite the opposite.

They are broad, multifarious, and often even seemingly contradictory.

The insistence of our culture, however, has been toward those narrow and precise concepts after the mathematical model. The long-standing debate concerning the concept of faith is a good example of that cultural pressure to eliminate what we conceive as contradictions and establish clear and simple concepts upon which to found our understanding. Central to the debate over the nature of faith is the question of whether faith is a propositional belief based in, and supported by, reason; or a desire or passion ultimately rooted in hope. The first position was especially popular with the Enlightenment thinkers of the seventeenth and eighteenth centuries. John Locke takes such a stance, and although he says that faith goes beyond reason and allows us to accept as true things for which reason gives us no direct evidence, when we examine such a position, we see that such faith, which takes us beyond reason, is ultimately rooted in reason.

In distinguishing reason from faith, Locke says that reason is

> the discovery of the certainty or probability of such propositions or truths . . .
> got by the use of its natural faculties. . . . Faith, on the other side, is the assent
> to any proposition . . . upon the credit of the proposer. (Locke IV. xviii. 2)

But the assent to a proposition based upon the credit of the proposer must ultimately rest in the fact that our natural faculties tell us that the credibility of a particular proposer, and what she is proposing, is probable. That is, with such an understanding of faith, we must ask why we believe a particular proposition based upon the testimony of one proposer and not the testimony of another? It cannot be because we have "faith" in the one and not the other, because that would require yet another proposer whose credibility we accept. In fact, we accept the testimony of one and not another because our natural faculties (i.e., reason) tell us that one is credible and the other is not. So although faith allows us to accept the testimony of others, and thus takes us beyond what we can know with our natural faculties alone, that faith must itself be founded upon our reasoning that a particular proposer's testimony is credible. Hence, even when we act in faith, it is ultimately based in reason. Our natural faculties tell us that dead people stay dead, but we believe the apostolic witness that Jesus had risen, because we reason that they are credible witnesses. Thus, our faith ultimately rests upon the credibility and number of the witnesses that attest to his resurrection.

In contrasts to this view of faith as a propositional belief supported in reason, some have argued that faith is rather a desire or passion ultimately rooted in hope. Kierkegaard says,

> Faith is a miracle, and yet no man is excluded from it; for that in which all human life is unified is passion, and faith is a passion. (Kierkegaard 77)

For Kierkegaard, the passion that is faith is close to what we might call hope.[1] This emotive view of faith stands in dire contrast to the cognitive view we first considered, and yet there are instances of Scripture which seem to support both. In the ninth chapter of Mark's Gospel, a man asks Jesus to cast out an evil spirit from his son.

> "But if You can do anything, take pity on us and help us!" And Jesus said to him, "'If You can!' All things are possible to him who believes." Immediately the boy's father cried out and began saying, "I do believe; help my unbelief." (Mark 9:22-24 NAS)

It would seem that the faith this man has is largely rooted in a desire or hope rather than in any reasoned confidence in the proposition, "All things are possible to him who believes," because Jesus is the one saying it. We have no indication that the man is a follower of Jesus or even knows much about him.

By contrast, the disciples' faith in this same situation is rooted more in reason than in hope. It is not their son who is seeking healing, and the disciples have experienced

---

1. Kierkegaard himself says that faith is not synonymous with hope but it is certainly a passion which has its roots in hope.

multiple instances of Jesus' ability and willingness to work miracles. Thus, their faith is more a matter of reason, while the faith of the boy's father is much more a matter of hope.

But what is the essential nature of faith? Is it a belief founded in reason, or is it a desire rooted in hope? Based upon what is given in Scripture, it would seem to be both. Indeed, in addition to the example given in Mark 9:22-24, there are many more biblical instances of faith, some of which are clearly a reasoned confidence in a proposition based on the credit of the proposer, while others are much more a matter of hope. The faith of a mature Moses or David is largely based upon the fact that they had heard from God time and time again, and what he said was to be trusted. Their faith is largely of the first type, but the faith of someone like Rahab seems to be more of the second type.

So at times faith seems to be of one nature, and at other times it seems to be of a completely different nature. But how can faith be both a desire rooted in hope and a belief supported in reason? The fact that we have difficulty conceptualizing faith as both emotive and cognitive seems to result from a certain error in our thinking about concepts in general. The error can be traced to Aristotle, but he is neither the sole source of the error, nor is he solely responsible for it having become so entrenched in Western thought. He does, however, provide a good point of focus in order to address the conceptual error which prevents us from properly understanding faith as it is set forth by the scriptural instances.

The error involves the way we form concepts in general. Aristotle argued that, in order to have a clear concept that would represent a kind of thing, we need to combine the genus of that kind of thing with its differentia (*Metaphysics*, VII, 12, and *Post. Analytics* II, 13, 96b15-97b39). To establish a clear concept of the species "human," we need to combine the genus "animal" and the differentia, those things which distinguish humans from other animals – for example, that they are rational. Thus, the concept "human" is understood as rational animal. In this model, a concept belongs to a single genus, and although Aristotle did allow for the possibility of a concept having two genuses (*Post. Analytics*, 97b7-26), the ideal is always that of a single genus. In Western thought, we have closely followed this model, and the taxonomies of our present biological science provide a good example of just how much this Aristotelian assumption dominates our thinking. In biology, we classify and conceptualize species under a single lineage whereby species of animals or plants belong to only one genus, one order, one class, one phylum, etc. Such ordering gives us neat and clear concepts and satisfies our desire to organize our experience in ways that make our understanding as clear as possible. At first this might seem natural, a right way to form concepts, but the truth is that many of our concepts, including faith, do not easily lend themselves to being conceptualized under a single genus.

In the *Symposium*, Socrates gives us the example of *eros*, which he argues is best understood as belonging to two genuses, rather than one. The idea of *eros* as descending from two very different genuses is allegorized with a story about the birth of *eros*.

> On the day of Aphrodite's birth the gods were making merry, and among them was Resource, son of Craft. And when they had supped, Need came begging at the door because there was good cheer inside. Now it happened that Resource, having drunk deeply of the heavenly nectar -- for this was before the days of wine -- wandered out into the garden of Zeus and sank into a heavy sleep, and Need, thinking that to get a child by Resource would mitigate her penury, lay down beside him and in time was brought to bed of Love. So Love became the follower and servant of Aphrodite because he was begotten on the same day that she was born. . . .
>   Then again, as the son of Resource and Need, it has been his fate to be always needy; nor is he delicate and lovely as most of us believe, but harsh and arid, barefoot and homeless, sleeping on the naked earth, in doorways, or in the very streets beneath the stars of heaven, and always partaking of his mother's poverty. But secondly, he brings his father's resourcefulness to his designs upon the beautiful and good, for he is gallant, impetuous, and energetic, a mighty hunter, and a master of device and artifice. (Plato, *Symposium* 203b1-203d7)

Thus, in Socrates' view, *eros* or erotic passion is not a species of pure want and desire, but neither is it a species of satisfaction and contentment. Instead, *eros* must be understood as somehow in the middle, having characteristics of both want and satisfaction. Socrates compares it to philosophy, which also must have its descent from a dual origin and be a member of two genuses. Indeed, philosophy must have a basis in ignorance, otherwise it would not desire knowledge; but it cannot be completely ignorant, or it would not know what to seek. It must thus share in the two very different genuses of ignorance and wisdom (Plato, *Symposium* 203e-204b9).

This view of a concept being a member of multiple genuses is certainly not the prevalent understanding which has dominated Western thought. Our thinking has very much sided with Aristotle on this point, and we find it difficult to imagine a species with more than a single genus. Consequently, in spite of the fact that faith, as it is presented in Scripture, more resembles Plato's concept of *eros* by seeming to be rooted both emotively and cognitively, our culture maintains the contrary Aristotelian perspective.

At least part of the reason behind the dominance of this view is that, in the modern era, the world came to be conceived of as a machine. In the seventeenth century a host of influential figures including Isaac Newton, Robert Boyle, Rene Descartes, John Locke, and Galileo, just to mention a few, came to embrace what was then known as the corpuscular philosophy and later came to evolve into what we know today as atomic chemistry. With this new mechanical view, many thinkers believed that the real essence and cause of a thing was its microscopic, internal structure. But that microscopic real essence of a thing, was unknown in the seventeenth century. Thus, the nominal essences that were used to group things into species or kinds, and to which the names of species were attached were not the real essences of things, but instead were mere abstract ideas created by human judgment from among the sense qualities that we do experience. Of course, the real essence or internal structure did create the sense qualities that we observe and from which we form our abstract idea or concept of the nominal essence (Locke III. iii. 15).

Today we have inherited an evolved version of this philosophy, and we maintain that the real essence and ultimate constitution of a thing like gold or water is its internal atomic or molecular structure; we believe that the sense qualities we observe, and from which we make up our abstract ideas or concept of something like gold (i.e., it being malleable, metallic, and gold in color), are the product of that internal structure. Therefore, what is truly essential about gold is not a certain composite of sense qualities, but the internal or atomic structure that is the cause of those qualities. Most importantly, we equally suppose that this microscopic internal structure which causes the sense qualities that make up the nominal essences is singular and not multiple. That is, we suppose a single real essence rather than a plurality of internal structures as the cause of the qualities from which we make up our concept of the nominal essence. But why do we suppose a single essence or cause? It seems we do so because we believe this process to be mechanical. If the way we think about the universe follows the model of the machine, we have a model that suggests linear and singular causal origins. With a machine, the movement of a gear is not sometimes caused by one thing and at other times by another thing, unless there is such a regular pattern built into the machine. In almost all cases, a machine's movements are regular, fixed, and linear. So if the world is mechanical, it is natural to suppose a regular, fixed, and linear chain of causes behind all that we observe and conceptualize. But is the world a machine, and are there single causes behind what we conceptualize? Equally, must our concepts be neatly tied to origins in single genuses? Conceptualizing our experience in such a linear way makes it difficult to understand something like faith as it is set forth by the biblical instances. Unfortunately, we seem to side with the overwhelming cultural influence on this matter, rather than the perspective offered by the biblical instances.

Because of our cultural prejudice toward forming concepts that are members of single genuses, and our prejudice that things originate from singular causes, we find it natural to suppose that a specific disease is a member of a single genus and has a singular cause, even when we do not know the internal cause of the disease. But it is clearly wrong to suppose that the nominal essence or abstract concept we create out of our own judgment, and to which we attach the name of the disease, should be a member of a single genus or have a single cause. There is no reason to believe this other than Aristotle has given us a model to think this way, and the mechanical view of the modern period has reinforced that thinking. Of course, the great appeal of the Aristotelian/Enlightenment model is that it gives us neat and clear concepts from which to organize our experience. The drawback to this model is that our experience often refuses to be organized according to such neat and clear concepts.

There have long been those who realized this and resisted the temptation to follow the Aristotelian/Enlightenment model. In the seventeenth century, Leibniz stood in opposition to the mechanical view and its idea of singular causes.

> There is an infinity of figures and movements, past and present, which contribute to the efficient cause of my presently writing this. And there is an infinity of minute inclinations and dispositions of my soul, which contribute to the final cause of my writing. (Leibniz 36)

In our day, Michel Foucault has argued against singular causal origins and has pointed to the model of genealogy as an alternative. Unlike the model of the machine, whose causal chain is linear, a genealogical model acknowledges a multitude of causes or ancestors. If genealogy, rather than the machine, was the model for our thinking about the genuses and causes behind our concepts, we would be open to form concepts that were members of multiple genuses and could be traced to multiple causes. Because of our conceptual prejudices, however, we find such conceptualizations difficult, and we all too easily follow the dominant model of our culture.

We suppose a singular cause behind our idea of race, just as we do in the case of diseases. Even though such concepts are clearly nominal and of our own creation, we imagine that there must be some phenotypical or genotypical characteristic that causes someone to be of one race rather than another. We imagine this because of our cultural attachment to an Aristotelian/Enlightenment model, yet clearly the physical characteristics from which we derive our idea of race are the result of human beings having a multitude of ancestors, not from having a single racial descent. Of course, if the causes of our physical characteristics are not the product of a single origin, but have origins as numerous as our ancestors, it would be impossible to say exactly what one's race was, and the concept of race would be lost, as perhaps it well should be. Indeed, a concept that descends from a multitude of genuses or has an almost infinite number of causes is not a concept at all. But that is not to say that a concept must originate and thus be a member of a single genus. Many concepts could have roots in several genuses and still retain a conceptual integrity. Faith, as it is presented by the biblical instances, is certainly such a concept.

The initial stages of faith do seem to represent something close to what we would call hope, and, therefore, such faith can be thought of as emotive rather than cognitive. In time, however, that hope takes on substance and gains the support of reason. When it gains enough rational support, the belief is no longer thought to be supported by faith but rather is thought to be held as knowledge. Just as we no longer think of an oak tree as an acorn or a butterfly as a caterpillar, so too as faith moves closer to knowledge, we tend to identify it as cognitive, rather than emotive. Faith is thus a middle ground which bring together an emotive element like hope with something as cognitive as knowledge.

Knowledge, by its most widely held definition, is justified, true belief.[2] The justification that distinguishes known true beliefs from other true beliefs takes the form of a *logos* or rational account that explains how or why a belief is true. My belief that a seven will come up on the next roll of the dice may turn out to be true,

2. In 1963, Edmund Gettier's paper "Is Justified True Belief Knowledge" cast doubt on this definition by presenting counter examples in which justified, true beliefs are not knowledge. This began an ongoing search for additional conditions that would eliminate Gettier's counter examples. We will avoid this controversy and all the exceptional cases in which justified, true belief is not knowledge and instead explore the vast majority of cases in which justified, true belief is knowledge.

but that does not allow it to be considered something I knew because there is no *logos* to support the belief. By contrast, my belief that water is a composite of hydrogen and oxygen is not only a true belief, but one supported by an extensive *logos* which entails the whole of atomic chemistry. Without such a *logos*, our true opinions might be no more than lucky guesses. Thus, the essential element which establishes a true belief as knowledge is this *logos*.

Of course, a big question is how much of a *logos* is required to make a true belief stand as knowledge? How extensive does the account have to be, or how much warrant is required in order to turn a true belief into knowledge? The answer to this question seems to be that knowledge is not a fixed point as it had been when "to know" meant "to be certain." If there is such a thing as probable knowledge, and some beliefs are more justified or have a greater degree of warrant than others as a greater probability accompanies them, so too there must be degrees concerning knowledge claims based upon how extensive and acceptable a *logos* or justification is.

At the other end of the scale, many beliefs are held without any supportive *logos* or justifying account. Much of what we came to believe as children was received unconsciously or at least unreflectively. Many people continue as adults to hold a large portion of their beliefs in a similar way. It is often said that they accept such beliefs on faith. But beliefs held in faith are not beliefs that are casually held or without support. Rather they are beliefs held in confidence because they do have support, though that support is not in the form of a *logos*. Instead, beliefs held in faith are supported and rooted in hope, which is not a belief about a state of affairs the way faith is, but a desire that a certain possible state of affairs would be realized.

Of course, it is possible to have a confidence in the truth of a belief that is neither supported by a *logos* nor hope. A person may have a confidence that a certain disaster will take place, but they hope that their belief will not be realized. In such cases the cause of their confidence is despair rather than hope.

So faith, or a confidence of belief, may exist without hope, and equally, hope is not always accompanied by faith. We may have a hope that is little more than a wish with little prospect of it being realized. A wish need not involve possibility, while a hope does require that the thing hoped for is at least remotely possible. Faith, on the other hand, is much more than the belief that a state of affairs is remotely possible. When faith is added, hope takes on a reality that it would otherwise not possess. Faith gives substance to hope (Heb. 11:1). Thus, faith is a conscious confidence in the truth of a belief even when there is little or no apparent warrant or supporting *logos*.

Truth then is a necessary ingredient in both faith and knowledge. Beliefs we hold as knowledge will be abandoned if they lose the element of truth. The Ptolemaic notion of a geocentric universe no longer stands as knowledge in spite of its supporting *logos*, because that supporting *logos* lost the essential element of truth. With Copernicus and the alternative *logos* he provided, a choice had to be made. Only one of the competing accounts would be granted a claim to truth. When the Copernican account was chosen, the Ptolemaic account lost its claim to truth.

Equally, if I have faith in my baseball team and hold the belief that they will win the championship, I maintain the truth of that belief. If by the end of the season, however, the facts are contrary to my belief, I can no longer hold to that belief because its truth has been lost (for that season anyway).

But while truth is a necessary ingredient in knowledge and faith, what distinguishes faith from knowledge is that with knowledge the necessary truth element is supplied by a *logos* or rational account which serves as reasonable evidence for the truth of the belief. With faith, the truth element, at least initially, is supplied by hope, and no immediate explanation of why something is true needs to be given. Of course, our tendency is to want to add a *logos* in order to give our beliefs support from more than mere hope. All beliefs held in faith have a natural dynamic whereby they go from being initially supported in hope to being supported in some sort of rational justification. If the supporting *logos* becomes extensive enough, the hope which initially supported the belief will disappear entirely. This often occurs in the sciences, and a belief held in faith today will be held as knowledge tomorrow as we are able to add a *logos* and give a sufficient account which explains why our belief is true. When a scientist pursues a particular hypothesis rather than a host of others, his belief is supported by a confidence that what he hopes for is true. It is, however, a temporary faith, for the scientist's ambition is that his belief would ultimately be supported entirely in a rational account, absent of the emotive support of hope.

But even when a belief becomes entirely supported by a *logos*, its initial support was a faith or confidence that originated in hope. Our elementary beliefs out of which we form the beliefs which make up a *logos* and provide a justification for our beliefs cannot themselves have a *logos* to support them. Since they are elementary, there cannot be a more elementary *logos* which might serve as their support (Plato, *Theaetetus*, 201e-202c).[3] Thus, initially our confidence in such beliefs must be rooted in hope.

This is the nature of the faith that is set forth in Scripture, but it is also the nature of faith in general and can be seen at work in all those who pursue knowledge, whether a personal knowledge of God or a philosophic/scientific knowledge of the world. Many philosophers of the past demonstrate that the path to knowledge begins in hope and proceeds through faith until knowledge is finally achieved. Even among those who are generally considered to be the most rational of philosophers, we see that they begin their quest of knowledge in an initial belief that is rooted in hope and faith.

In the *Meno*, Meno suggests to Socrates that learning is impossible because, as Socrates paraphrases,

> He would not seek what he knows, for since he knows it there is no need of the inquiry, nor what he does not know, for in that case he does not even know what he is to look for. (Plato, *Meno* 80E)

---

3. The basic beliefs which foundationalists claim need no justification will be addressed later in this chapter.

Socrates' immediate answer is the famous recollection myth in which he explains that the soul "is immortal and has been born many times, and has seen all things both here and in the other world" (Plato, *Meno* 81C). Thus, learning is possible because it is in fact no more than a mere recollection of what we have forgotten. Socrates then gives a demonstration in which he uses Meno's slave: he claims that the slave, who had never learned any geometry in this life, is able to come to a knowledge of geometry by recollecting or remembering the principles of geometry which he must have known at some point prior to this life.

Meno is impressed and takes the myth and its demonstration to prove that truth is in the soul and therefore knowledge is possible. Socrates, on the other hand, although he says that he also believes that truth is in the soul, indicates that he is not as sure as Meno. What he is certain of, however, is that we should act as if knowledge were possible.

> Meno: Somehow or other I believe you are right.
> Socrates: I think I am. I shouldn't like to take an oath on the whole story, but one thing I am ready to fight for as long as I can, in word and act – that is, that we shall be better, braver, and more active men if we believe it is right to look for what we don't know than if we believe there is no point in looking because what we don't know we can never discover. (Plato, *Meno* 86B-C)

So it seems that Socrates' belief that knowledge is possible is not so much based upon a *logos* (i.e., the recollection myth and its demonstration with the slave boy) as it is a hope that such a belief will give us certain desired values (i.e., to be braver and better men). Of course, the other value that motivates our hope in such a belief is knowledge itself. We believe that knowledge is valuable or a good that will make life meaningful, so we put our faith in those elementary beliefs which we hope will lead to knowledge.

This seems to be the case with Descartes as well. In the *Discourse on Method*, he explains his discovery of the method that led him to knowledge. Of course, this discovery cannot itself be knowledge or a part of knowledge. Existing prior to knowledge, it must be something other than knowledge, and that something looks very much like what we have been calling hope and faith.

Descartes tells us that his famous first principle "I think, therefore I am" was discovered simply by doubting everything until he came to this one truth that was completely beyond doubt. But this first piece of knowledge was preceded by a method which could not have been entered into in the knowledge that it would lead him to his desired end, but in the hope and faith that it would.

Additionally, in part three of the *Discourse on the Method* (Descartes' famous "cogito" is presented in part four), he sets forth a series of provisional maxims to be used until he can gain knowledge. His second maxim, he says,

> was that of being as firm and resolute in my actions as I could be, and not to follow less faithfully opinions the most dubious, when my mind was once made up regarding them, than if these had been beyond doubt. (Descartes 96)

He then says this is a maxim "very true and very certain" (Descartes 96). But if it is a maxim "very true and very certain," that truth is not a truth that comes out of his philosophy or follows from his first principle of the *cogito*, for indeed it precedes both. In fact, it is a belief, like the one that Socrates is willing to fight for, that precedes all knowledge and is based upon a hope and faith that such a belief will give us what we want. Socrates believes it will make us better by making us "braver, and more active men." Descartes believes something very close to that: such a maxim will

> deliver me from all the penitence and remorse which usually affect the mind and agitate the conscience of those weak and vacillating creatures . . . . (Descartes 96)

Thus, for both Socrates and Descartes, the value or good they wish to pursue is knowledge, and in both cases they see resolute action as a means to that good. Of course, a belief that resolute action will lead to knowledge cannot be supported by knowledge, but it can be supported by a hope that such a belief is a means to knowledge. Our confidence in our initial beliefs is almost always supported entirely by hope.

This is true throughout all of philosophy and science. Every system or body of knowledge must begin with a step of faith in the hope that such a step will eventually lead to knowledge. Whether our first steps are in the direction of sense experience or steps toward the *a priori* truths of logic and mathematics, they must always be steps of faith based upon hope. To get started on the path to knowledge, we need to take a step of faith and put our confidence either in the laws of identity and contradiction or in the belief that our senses are reliable and accurately inform us concerning reality. At this elementary stage, the support for that confidence must be found largely in hope.

Of course, today's foundationalists maintain that a belief in sense data is a basic belief and needs no justification. Even if this is true, however, it is hard to imagine how our conceptual understanding of the world can be directly traced to sense data. True, sense data may be *a* basis for our perceptions, but these perceptions are also formed by our conceptual understanding of the world, which is largely cultural and varies from one language community to another. "In short, perceptual recognition and identification involve the employment of concepts" (Landesman 621), and concepts are not solely the product of sense data.

Since even our most elementary and foundational beliefs are conceptual, they do need justification. But what could be the justification for such foundational beliefs? It would seem that any confidence we place in them would have to rest in the hope that such beliefs would serve as a foundation that would allow for a body of empirical knowledge. The logical positivists' notion that we should accept nothing as meaningful unless it can be verified or falsified in observation is meaningless by its own criterion. If such a belief is to be meaningful, it must be because we hope that placing our confidence in such a supposition will lead us to the kind of knowledge we desire.

The same is true of the rationalist claim to knowledge based upon the laws of identity and contradiction. A equals A, and A does not equal not A. But why? To say that A does not equal not A because of the law of contradiction is to beg the question. We cannot use the law of contradiction to prove the law of contradiction. Any rational account begs the question and supposes the very principle we are trying to establish. The only answer that does not beg the question is that our confidence in the law of contradiction is supported by the hope that such a foundational belief will lead to a body of *a priori* knowledge. Believing that the certainty which *a priori* knowledge yields is good, and seeing that the laws of identity and contradiction are a necessary first step toward that good, we support such primary beliefs with a faith that this thing in which we have placed our hope will lead us to what we desire. Thus, the rationalist, as well as the empiricist, must go outside of her own criterion and establish her initial beliefs in hope.

This fact that our beliefs are ultimately rooted in hope should not be taken to mean that our beliefs are not based in some sort of reasoning. Although hope may be the original root of our foundational beliefs, it is not their only root. Sound beliefs gain support from reasonable evidence, and a rational account begins to develop. Unsound beliefs lack such additional roots and eventually wither, or they must be supported by pure tenacity. So to say that beliefs are ultimately rooted in hope is not to deny reasonable evidence as a basis for our beliefs. It is rather to say that beliefs have multiple roots. The original root may be hope, but without additional rational roots that provide a body or evidence, hope alone is unable to sustain the belief for long.

All justifiable beliefs are of this kind to one extent or another, and go from being supported almost exclusively in hope to being ever more supported in some type of reason. Not all beliefs are capable of becoming so exclusively a matter of knowledge that they are supported entirely in reason and need no support from hope, but all beliefs move in that direction and gain rational support, or they are abandoned.

Thus, in spite of our tendency to think that faith must be either emotive or rational, the fact is that faith, especially our faith in God, is rooted in both hope and knowledge and is both emotive and cognitive. The basis of our faith, or confidence in our beliefs, is not singular, but originates in hope and then dynamically moves toward knowledge. Faith is not something that is static and can be pinned down to an essence which descends from a single genus, but rather it is a dynamic middle ground between hope and knowledge. We seek to "know" God -- a knowledge of him is the end toward which we move, but the means to that knowledge always comes through a faith that originates in hope.

When two people marry, they may have faith in each other, but that faith is initially little more than a hope. In time, that faith may become more than mere hope as one person proves faithful and gives reason for the other person to trust him. Our beliefs about the trustworthiness of people are always of this type. My belief that Harry will be trustworthy tomorrow in a certain situation will never be supported by the kind of conclusive *logos* that makes a belief stand purely as knowledge. It will always be a faith based to a large extent upon hope, but my faith does become more rational as the person in whom I place my faith gives me good reason to trust him.

Our belief in the faithfulness of God is certainly an instance of this kind of personal faith. It may begin as a confidence based in little more than hope, but in time, as God continues to demonstrate his faithfulness, our faith and confidence find its support in a knowledge of him and his faithfulness.

Thus, unlike my faith that a seven will be rolled with the next throw of the dice, which will forever be supported purely by hope,[4] my faith in God is a faith in a person and, as such, is capable of gaining rational support as the trustworthiness of that person becomes known over time. Certainly the amount of evidence that supports my belief in another person varies with the person and my experiences of him, and it will never amount to that degree of certainty that would entirely eliminate hope from the equation. Still, the more evidence I have, the greater my claim to knowing that

---

4. Of course, it is possible for one to do a probability study, in which case the roll of the dice would be more than mere hope.

person.

Additionally, in the case of God, as with any person, there is a continual movement back toward hope as we find ourselves in new situations where we lack a knowledge of his faithfulness. In time, if we give God opportunity in those situations, we do see his faithfulness, and our confidence in him becomes more a matter of knowledge than hope in those areas as well. Another new situation in which we lack a knowledge of God and his faithfulness, however, will cause our faith to fall back again upon hope. But in spite of this seemingly backward movement, there is an ongoing strengthening of our faith as evidence of God's faithfulness gives us additional support for our confidence in him. Our faith truly is from God in that he gives us ever more reason to believe and trust in him. Thus, although our faith in God may begin emotively in the passion that is hope, his faithfulness provides the rational support that we naturally seek. Thus, the Scripture rightly says that our faith rests both within our hope in him (Ps. 43:5 and Ps. 78:7) and our knowledge of him (Hos. 2:20 and Col. 1:10).

Since faith has two very different supports (i.e., the emotive and rational), it will vary from individual to individual, and even possibly within the same individual in different situations, depending upon the distinct combination of emotive and rational elements that make up the individual's faith in a particular situation. One element is not better than the other, and the only dangerous faith is either one so intent upon the passion of hope that it does not desire increased rational support in the knowledge of God, or the one that is exclusively founded upon knowledge to the exclusion of hope – indeed, the demons may know that God is all powerful, but their hope is that he is not (Jas. 2:19). The faith that God would have for us -- the faith prescribed by the Scriptural instances -- is a faith that is founded upon a hope in God and a desire to know him ever more.

Chapter 7

The Concept of a Miracle

Sometimes it is especially difficult to reconstruct our concepts after God's intentional meaning because the instances or extensions of the concept are especially misleading or deceptive due to our cultural bias. This appears to be the case with our concept of miracles. Our culture basically provides two possible alternative conceptualizations of miracles. The one chooses to see all sorts of events as extensions of the spectacular and miraculous, while the other chooses to conceptualize miracles as illusionary phenomena which appeal to feeble minds. In our secular age, many people maintain this latter position, but such a view is also popular among many of today's religious people who maintain that the age of miracles is past.

Two philosophers who have often been associated with these two opposing positions on miracles are Jonathan Edwards (1703 -1758) and David Hume (1711 - 1776). Although contemporaries of one another, the two men are generally thought to represent two antithetical views on miracles. It is typical to consider Hume to be an antagonist of the Christian faith and opposed to miracles and the supernatural, while Edwards, as one of the leaders of The Great Awakening, is generally taken to be a great defender of the miraculous and supernatural. Yet when examined, both men seem similar to each other in their conceptualization of what is and is not a miracle. Furthermore, this shared position is different from the two dominant cultural views, but does seem to reflect both the biblical instances as well as a liberal (almost postmodern) perspective concerning our conceptualization of something like a miracle.

Hume's most noted position on miracles is set forth in the essay, "Of Miracles" which appears as Section X of *An Inquiry Concerning Human Understanding*. The book, like most of Hume's work, truly is an inquiry into human understanding, and throughout that inquiry Hume continually comes to the conclusion that human understanding is not based as much on reason as his predecessors and contemporaries had believed. Much of our understanding, Hume was to claim, was based in certain customs which arise out of psychological habits and sentiments rather than reason. Throughout the inquiry, Hume continually finds that our understanding is more customary and emotive than rational. This is no less true concerning our understanding of Christianity, which Hume thought was not based in reason but in an inward, emotive experience that is "brought home to everyone's breast by the immediate operation of the Holy Spirit" (Hume, *Inquiry* 117). Many of Hume's critics take his reference to the Holy Spirit to be disingenuous, but such a statement is consistent with the rest of Hume's philosophy. Since the sentiments that we feel within our breast are what lie at the base of his moral philosophy, it is natural that such an inward, emotive experience would lie at the base of any genuine religious faith as well. If our understanding in general is largely emotive and sentimental, rather than rational, why wouldn't our understanding of Christianity be the same? Or, to take it a step further, why wouldn't true miracles be based in sentiment rather than reason?

Such a position is not unlike the one Kierkegaard took a century later. Like

Kierkegaard, Hume thinks that genuine religious belief, as well as a belief in miracles, is based in some inward experience or aesthetic sentiment. Thus, Hume is not taking a position in opposition to Christianity (though he is certainly in opposition to the dominant rational theology of his day) but rather a position which opposes reason as the basis of the Christian faith. Just as Hume had shown earlier in the *Inquiry* that reason was an insufficient basis for our understanding of cause and effect, in the chapter "Of Miracles" he shows it is also an insufficient basis for the Christian faith and for a belief in miracles.

Throughout the *Inquiry*, Hume continually shows the shortcomings of reason – that it does not provide the basis for our understanding which nearly everyone in his day believed it did. Furthermore, he even shows that it is capable of leading us into error. In Section X ("Of Miracles"), Hume tells us that the Indian prince reasoned justly in rejecting the reports he received concerning frost. Of course, the reports were true, but it was still reasonable to reject them because the reports were so contrary to the experience the prince had accumulated over the course of his lifetime. The implication is that it is not always best to follow reason because it is not an infallible guide nor is it our only guide. This certainly contrasts with the dominant medieval view, which held that the emotions lead us into error while reason leads us into truth. With such a view, the course is simple – follow reason, and avoid being lead by the emotions.

Hume was opposed to such a view. Reason was not the rock solid basis of our understanding, and emotive sentiments were more to be trusted than his predecessors had thought. Certainly, emotive sentiments are not infallible; since they are molded and shaped by custom and convention, they are imperfect guides, but, nevertheless, they represent the true basis for our understanding, and can be trusted (Livingston 22).

The fact that Hume points to a sentiment rather than reason as the true basis of the Christian faith is no reason to think he is dismissing that faith. Just as he does not dismiss the idea of cause and effect or morality, and he does not refuse to be guided by them because he discovers that they are not based in reason, neither does he suggest dismissing Christianity because he finds it to be other than reason-based.

If religious faith, however, is only erroneously based in reason and is truly based in an inner feeling or sentiment, how can we be certain of our faith? But that is exactly Hume's point. Christianity is a matter of faith, not reason.

> Our most holy religion is founded on faith, not on reason; and it is a sure method of exposing it to put it to such a trial as it is by no means fitted to endure. (Hume, *Inquiry* 140)

So if we take Hume at his word, he is not opposed to Christianity but rather the reasonableness of Christianity. Unlike the other two British empiricists who preceded him and with whom he is often linked, Hume was not interested, as they were, to show the "reasonableness of Christianity." Locke had written a book by that title, and Berkeley held precisely the point that Hume was attacking – that it is reasonable to trust the apostolic witness concerning the miracles that Jesus had performed, and that such testimony is a sufficient basis for a rational faith.

> Appeal to eyewitness testimony for the biblical miracles is the heart of Berkeley's defence of the Christian religion. Berkeley maintains that miracles confirmed that Moses, the Apostles, and the other biblical witnesses talked with God. (Slupik 521)

Berkeley believed, as did most people of the day, that God has equipped us with reason in order that we might know him and the world in which he has placed us.

> We should believe that God has dealt more bountifully with the sons of men, than to give them a strong desire for that knowledge, which he had placed quite out of their reach. (Berkeley, Sect. 3)

Hume was opposed to such a view, holding that our knowledge does not extend nearly as far as we think. In Hume's view, God has not given us a capacity for knowledge in many areas, including Christianity. But this did not mean that a providential God has not equipped us with an ability to know him and the world in which he has placed us. The question is not whether God had equipped us, but how he has equipped us and to what extent. Many thinkers in Hume's day imagined that our God-given reason was capable of leading us to certainty or near certainty. Hume was undermining that view. He claimed that what we have been equipped with was not so much reason, as an ability to feel sentiments, make associations, and form habits. This, rather than knowledge in the strict sense, was the means with which we have been equipped in order to know God and the world in which he has placed us. Of course, with this view a certain freedom of judgment comes into play. Thus, we cannot always be sure of the origin and meaning of our sentiments, and the associations we make are sometimes mistaken or do not accurately represent the world as God intended it to be understood.

This perspective differs from the traditional view, which guaranteed a more exact understanding of the world. With a faith in reason, there could be a certain confidence in our understanding. Of course, Hume was attacking that position, and this seems to have been more his sin than an actual undermining of the Christian faith itself.

Another factor which added to Hume's infamous reputation was that he challenged the meaning of miracles themselves. Hume points out that what most people consider miracles are thought to be signs that something is from God (Hume, *Inquiry* 117). A sign is certainly something that points to something else, and miracles are often referred to as signs, but are miracles necessarily a sign that something is from God? Hume mentions "the many instances of forged miracles and prophecies and supernatural events" (Hume, *Inquiry* 126). Such bogus miracles signify, not that something is from God, but "the strong propensity of mankind to the extraordinary and marvelous" (Hume, *Inquiry* 126).

According to what Hume says, whether or not a miracle is from heaven is evidenced by the internal witness of the Holy Spirit (Hume, *Inquiry* 117), and not because of its spectacular nature. This seems consistent with Jesus' warning against setting our attention and hope upon the spectacular which so many consider miraculous. Jesus warns against a faith founded upon the miraculous when he says, "Except ye see signs and wonders, ye will not believe" (John 4:48 KJV), or "an evil and adulterous generation [that] seeketh after a sign" (Matt. 12:39 KJV). Of course, Jesus did perform miracles, but he never did a miracle in response to a request for a sign. The Jewish authorities often desired that Jesus would give them a sign. That is, they wanted a miracle which they claimed would be a sign that Jesus' authority was divine. But what they considered a miracle in itself is no more than a sign of the spectacular, and Jesus did not seem interested in gratifying their desire for the spectacular.

> And when Herod saw Jesus, he was exceeding glad: for he was desirous to see him of a long season, because he had heard many things of him; and he hoped to have seen some miracle done by him. (Luke 23:8 KJV)

This is not to say that miracles are not meaningful and cannot be a basis for the Christian faith. Hume's point is rather that the miracles which serve as the basis for the Christian faith are not the spectacular occurrences which most recognize as miraculous, but are sentiments which are "brought home to everyone's breast by the immediate operation of the Holy Spirit" (Hume, *Inquiry* 117).

This understanding of Hume's concerning the miraculous is similar to the explanation that Jonathan Edwards offered concerning the apparently miraculous manifestations that were taking place during The Great Awakening. Like Hume, Edwards warned against basing one's faith on an outward manifestation that appeared supernatural or miraculous. To Edwards, the strange behavior people were exhibiting during the Great Awakening were not at all supernatural, but were merely psychological responses to what God was supernaturally doing inside the person (Miller 169-70). Like Hume, Edwards points to what is going on inside the person. Like Hume, Edwards looks to the emotive as the genuine basis for religious experience and the miraculous. Like Hume, Edwards saw that there was an emotive element in human experience which was not something to be shunned or avoided but was in fact what enriched human experience and in many cases was a reliable guide. Both Edwards and Hume, although being men of reason, understood that reason was not the whole story and that the emotions had a large role to play.

Such a stand placed both Edwards and Hume at odds with two huge camps, both of which exalted reason and demeaned the emotions. On the one side, many of their contemporaries held to a medieval theology that saw the affections as a source of evil. They maintained that reason was good and from God, and therefore the affections, being the opposite of reason, must be evil. On the other side stood those who embraced the Enlightenment notion that reason simply was all-sufficient and there was no need for the emotive.

Edwards, in opposition to both his medieval and Enlightenment adversaries, believed that an emotive element made up a large part of true religion.

> A great part of true religion lies in the affections.
> It may be inquired, what the affections of the mind are.
>   I answer: The affections are no other than the more vigorous and sensible exercises of the inclination and will of the soul.
>   God has endued the soul with two faculties: one is that by which it is capable of perception and speculation, or by which it discerns, and views, and judges of things; which is called the understanding. The other faculty is that by which the soul does not merely perceive and view things, but is some way inclined with respect to the things it views or considers; either is inclined *to* them, or is disinclined and averse *from* them; or is the faculty by which the soul does not behold things as an indifferent unaffected spectator, but either as liking or disliking, pleased or displeased, approving or rejecting. (Edwards, *Religious Affections* 24)

For Edwards, Christianity was more than merely a set of rational or cognitive beliefs. More important was how one felt about what she understood.

> Any man could understand intellectually what a verse in the Bible or a doctrine of theology said, but not all could feel what it meant. (Miller 65)

Both Edwards and Hume had accepted Locke's notion that the affections could
be traced to "simple ideas, which we receive both from *Sensation* and *Reflection*"
(Locke II. xx. 1). In Locke's epistemology there was no separation between the
emotive and the rational at least in the sense that if all we can know are ideas, then the
emotions are ideas, which, like all ideas, can be traced ultimately to experience.
Locke believed that both pleasure and pain were simple ideas arising from the senses,
and that all other emotions were modifications of those simple ideas of pleasure or
pain. This is close to Hume's position.

> I believe it may safely be establish'd for a general maxim, that no object is
> presented to the senses, nor image form'd in the fancy, but what is
> accompany'd with some emotion. (Hume, *Treatise* 373)

The experience that gives us our ideas of emotions is a "kind of inward tasting or
feeling, of sweetness or pleasure, bitterness or pain, that is implied in it, or arises from
it" (Miller 159). This statement refers to Edwards' position, but it could equally be
attributed to Hume or Locke. All three men believed in experience as the origin of
all ideas, including the affections. In fact, much of Hume's work is an attempt to
show that many of our ideas, when traced, have their origin in an emotive idea rather
than a sense image.

The big question is this: what causes such an experience? Locke was a
corpuscularian and believed – as did Newton, Boyle, and so many other seventeenth
century thinkers – that the arrangement and motion of insensible corpuscles (later to
be known as atoms) were the source of all that we experience of the physical world,
but what of those inward, emotive sensations? Certainly emotions can be stimulated
chemically, but in other cases emotions seem to accompany certain experiences, as
Hume describes above. Equally, God could touch us in supernatural ways that could
stimulate emotions.

To complicate the matter still further, most emotions have a conceptual element
as well. A small child would not feel a sense of heroic awe in witnessing or thinking

about people giving their lives for some noble cause because the child lacks the conceptual framework that would be necessary for such an emotive experience. This conceptual element may be the most significant determinant concerning emotions, since

> a man is affected by – that is, he loves or hates – not things as they are in themselves, but things as he perceives them. (Miller 152-53)

Both Locke and Hume had shown that there was a considerable liberty concerning our conceptualization of the world which influences the meaning we attribute to our emotive experience, just as our conceptualization of the world influences the meaning we attribute to our experience in general. Our conceptualization of our emotive experience, however, is more complicated than our conceptualization of the physical world. With emotive experience there could be a variety of different stimuli, and what we judge the stimuli to be will have a great effect upon our conceptualization of the experience. Unlike physical experience, in which we can easily discern between being in a fire and imagining we are in a fire, it is not so easy to discern whether the stimulus of an emotive experience is the real world or the imagination, or whether the experience has an origin in the satanic or divine.

The determination of the source and meaning of various emotions was a real and pressing problem to Edwards. As one of the key figures of The Great Awakening, Edwards came under attack by those who held that the emotionalism which was associated with the movement was not of God. Edwards wanted to defend the fact that there was an emotive element to Christianity, but he did not want to defend all emotion as being from God. Edwards was well aware that the imagination was also involved in what people were experiencing.

> Of course, many have their heads full of imaginations, but that "does not prove that they have nothing else." (Miller 170)

In attempting to sort this out, Edwards agrees with his critics that all of the physical manifestations experienced by those individuals associated with The Great Awakening were a purely natural and psychological response to emotions rather than emotions themselves (Miller 169-70). Edwards argues that people naturally respond when they experience emotions and their response is neither the emotion itself nor is it any indication of the origin of the emotion. Using his Lockean model, Edwards separates the emotion itself (or pure experience), from our conceptualization of it and our physical reaction to it. Thus, the stimuli may be from God, but the conceptualization of it and the response to it are ours. With such a view, Edwards was able to maintain a middle ground whereby he could accept an emotive experience as being from God, without having to accept every human response to such emotions as a manifestation which was heaven sent.

Thus, having established that only the stimuli was from God and not our conceptualization and reaction to it, Edwards wanted to know how we can determine when the stimuli of an emotive experience is truly from God and when is it not? What he wanted to know was

> wherein those affections that are spiritual and gracious, do differ from those that are not so. (Edwards, *Religious Affections* 120)

It could never be that the origin of an emotion was determined by another emotion, since the question then would be what was the origin of that second confirming emotion, and the process of confirmation would extend to infinity. Edwards concludes that Scripture did offer guidelines by which we could judge emotive experiences. These Christ-given guidelines were not intended as a means to conclude with certainty which emotive experiences were of God and which were not.

> It was never God's design to give us any rules, by which we may certainly know, who of our fellow professors are his, and to make a full and clear separation between sheep and goats. (Edwards, *Religious Affections* 120)

It was God's purpose, however, to give

rules to all Christians, to enable them to judge of professors of religion, whom they are concerned with, so far as is necessary for their own safety, and to prevent their being led into a snare by false teachers, and false pretenders to religion. (Edwards, *Religious Affections* 120)

Edwards finds twelve such rules in Scripture. In the first of these rules, Edwards claims that

as to truly spiritual sensations, not only is the manner of its coming into the mind extraordinary, but the sensation itself is totally diverse from all that men have, or can have, in a state of nature. (Edwards, *Religious Affections* 141)

What Edwards is claiming is that with a true religious affection the simple ideas themselves are unlike anything we have ever experienced. If an impression upon our mind is of something we have already sensed, that impression could easily be the product of some demonic influence or our own imagination.

And if Satan or any created being, has power to impress the mind with outward representations, then no particular sort of outward representation can be any evidence of a divine power. (Edwards, *Religious Affections* 144)

And of the imagination, he says,

These imaginations do oftentimes raise the carnal affections of men to an exceeding great height: and no wonder, when the subjects of them have an ignorant, but undoubting persuasion that they are divine manifestations, which the great Jehovah immediately makes to their souls, therein giving them testimony in an extraordinary manner of His high and peculiar favor. (Edwards, *Religious Affections* 146)

If these natural impressions imposed upon the mind are less than true signs of divine affection, however, then so too would be those impressions that make up the miracles of which Hume was critical. Indeed, miracles, as they are commonly understood, are never of the supernatural nature that Edwards thinks identify true divine affections. For a miracle is an experience made up of the natural simple and complex ideas we normally experience with the exception that they are arranged differently than we have previously experienced them. For Edwards, what most consider a supernatural religious experience, such as a vision whereby someone beholds a "great outward light" or "Christ's hanging on the cross" (Edwards, *Religious Affections* 139), are not supernatural at all, since such experiences are made up of simple ideas that are common and mundane, and not the extraordinary simple ideas that make up true religious affection. For this reason, true religious affections are difficult or perhaps even impossible to describe with a language whose words have their reference and meaning based in natural sensations. Perhaps the most we can say of such true religious affections is that they are "the immediate operation of the Holy Spirit" (Hume, *Inquiry* 117).

Chapter 8

Toward a Postmodern
Correspondence Theory of Truth

According to the oldest and most widely held theory, truth exists as a correspondence between things and our ideas of them (*veritas est adaequatio rei et intellectus*). Now many of us may continue to cling to such a theory or definition of truth, but it has become increasingly difficult to maintain that such correspondence is a viable test for truth. Over the past few centuries, the widespread popularity of certain philosophies has made it ever more difficult for us to believe that a reality that exists apart from our ideas is knowable and thus capable of making our ideas true as they correspond to such a reality.

Locke had argued that the most we can ever know are ideas of things and never things themselves (Locke, IV. iii. 1), and Kant's *Critiques* were influential in convincing us that it is always our experience of things and not things themselves that are the objects of knowledge. With the twentieth century, the problem becomes further complicated by the fact that cultural anthropology and linguistic philosophies have brought us to understand that what is in our intellect is shaped by language, rather than by a direct experience of the world. If language shapes our intellect, the question then becomes this: how do we know if language correctly and univocally reflects objective reality. Since the world that language creates is highly conceptual, while the world apart from language is not conceptual, how can we establish a correspondence between that which is conceptual and that which is not conceptual? The traditional answer to these questions in a Western culture dominated by Christianity has been that a benevolent God would not deceive human beings and thus would equip us with the mental and linguistic hardware necessary to accurately reflect the world as he intended it to be understood.

Certainly, we are equipped with some type of hardware that allows us to form language and ideas which reflect our experience. The problem is that such equipment allows us to form language and ideas that reflect the perspectival nature of our experience which Nietzsche and William James were so adept at pointing out. Indeed, it even allows us to form ideas that reflect the historicity of our experience (e.g., Kuhn and Foucault), as well as the culturally relative nature of our experience as so many cultural anthropologists and linguistic philosophers have stressed. It would appear that our natural equipment allows us a liberty to form concepts that reflect the fullness of our human experience and not merely the brute facts of that experience.

Certainly, there are brute facts which we all commonly experience. These may be understood as the sense data that even brutes would experience if they had sense organs similar to our own. Such sense-based facts involve only a minimal amount of conceptualization, and therefore our ideas or statements about brute facts can be said to correspond, at least roughly, to things. My statement, "This thing (pointing to something) is closer to me than that thing (pointing to something else)," is true because of its correspondence to certain facts concerning "this thing" and "that thing" and their spatial relationship to me. A correspondence test for truth is appropriate in this case because "this thing" and "that thing" refer to actual things and not concepts.

Furthermore, the pronoun, "me," like a proper noun, refers to a thing and not a concept. The only real concept (with the exception of "the," "is," and "to") is distance, which seems to form naturally as the product of some sort of universal human hardware rather than out of a human freedom to make judgments and form conventional concepts. By contrast, the proposition, "That black person is a mammal," refers to concepts rather than things and, unlike the concept of "distance," the concepts of "black people" and "mammals" are conventional and the product of human judgment rather than a direct experience of the world. When our language and ideas do not refer to individual things but to concepts which are rooted in human judgment and conventions, to what are they to correspond? Since most language is conceptual, and most concepts are not the result of a natural or God-given hardware like the concept of "distance," but instead the result of human judgment and conventions, if the truth of those concepts is to be established by correspondence, it must be a correspondence to some other conceptualizing agent or agents. If that is the case, however, truth is no longer objective.

Kant, and others after him, have tried to overcome this difficulty by arguing that we are equipped with quite extensive hardware that serves to organize our sense data and supply us with concepts that are universal and common to all human beings. Today, however, most philosophers feel compelled to concede that most of the concepts which organize the brute facts of our experience into an understanding are not the product of a universal human hardware but are historically, culturally, and linguistically relative.

Certainly our conceptualization of people as either black or white is based upon certain brute facts which are given. But we are able to conceptualize people as black or white, only because our hardware offers us enough liberty to include the perspectival, historical, and cultural relativity of our experience. The concept of race, as we presently have it, is based in a choice to form one specific concept of race rather than multitudes of other possible concepts of race. It is even possible, given the same brute facts, to choose not to form a concept of race at all. Our formation of racial concepts, although based in the brute facts of our experience, involves a freedom concerning what aspects of the sense-based facts we choose to distinguish as essential.

This freedom of judgment and our ability to create alternative concepts accounts for the different perspectival, historical, and cultural conceptualization of our experience and, as we saw earlier, can readily be seen in a child's initial exposure to language and her first attempts at forming concepts. Often her initial concepts are different from the conventional concepts of her language community. Upon learning that the word *dog* is associated with her family's pet St. Bernard, and the word *cat* with their pet Siamese, an encounter with a Yorkshire Terrier would cause her to classify it with the small house pet, *cat*, rather than with the large house pet, *dog*.

In many cases, the brute facts of experience do not lead to the conventional concepts of our language communities in the way that our experience of distance leads us to a universal concept of distance. That occurs because most of our concepts are formed out of a combination of raw experience and judgment, and it is the liberty involved in our judgments that allows us to conceptualize our experience in a vast variety of ways. It is this liberty we have in forming our concepts that undermines a correspondence test for truth.

The Aristotelian medievals believed that we had a God-given ability to abstract essences and thus form concepts from what is given in the brute facts of experience. Certainly, we do have such an ability, which is in fact part of our imagination, and with it we can abstract an almost infinite number of such essences to form an equally infinite number of concepts. Given my experience of a telephone pole, my wife's mahogany rolling pin, and a dark wine bottle, I can abstract certain common characteristics and thus form the concept of "dark cylindrical." The abstraction of such a common essence, however, does not mean that such an essence establishes a concept that mirrors the world or even a universal human experience of it.

True, some concepts may arise purely out of experience with little liberty of judgment or imagination involved. Berkeley mentions the above example of distance (Berkeley, sects 42-43) which does seem to be a product of raw experience with little, if any, freedom of judgment involved in the experience. We experience the instances of distance and do not confuse them with instances of any other kind of experience. But that seems to be a rather rare exception, and with the vast majority of our concepts there are alternative possibilities that are equally viable, and our concepts result from both experience and judgment, rather than simple experience.

Thus, even if we were naturally equipped to form some concepts which inerrantly reflect a singular human experience (as in the case of distance), in most areas of our experience, we enjoy an enormous liberty concerning how we choose to group and conceptualize that experience. The very fact that our philosophical and scientific communities constantly divide the world into new and ever more refined concepts is further evidence of this freedom to conceptualize the world far beyond those few concepts that may form univocally among human beings. What has generated nominalism, historicism, perspectivalism, and ultimately the end of modernity, is a human freedom in regard to our conceptualization of the world. Because of this freedom of judgment that accompanies most of our experience, we have no way to get to the-thing-itself. That is, the thing apart from our conceptualization of it always escapes us and thus we have nothing for our ideas to correspond to. In light of this, it is difficult to imagine how correspondence could serve as a basis for truth. Since there is no way to step outside of our own relative conceptualization of the world, there is nothing with which to establish correspondence, and we are forced to accept a certain relativity concerning our understanding of the world.

Thus, although there might be the possibility of correspondence – inexact as it may be – between our ideas and the brute facts of the physical world, once those ideas of the brute facts are conceptualized, and organized into an understanding, there is no longer anything for them to correspond to. As we move further from the facts, and deeper into the world of our understanding, things become enormously relative because of the liberty we have to conceptualize the world as we choose. Because of this, the truth of the conceptual reality of our day is often established on a basis of how well a certain conceptualization offers a coherent picture of the phenomena we are considering and/or how well a particular conceptualization yields the pragmatic consequences we value. The truth of atomic chemistry rests in the fact that it provides a coherent explanation of the microcosmic world, and it provides us with the ability to mathematize and predict what happens in the microcosmic world, which is something we highly value.

In addition to this conceptual problem which prevents a correspondence to objective reality or an objective state of affairs, there is also the problem of valuation. Concerning propositions which involve values such as "the rose is beautiful," "it is good to be just," or "all men should be equal under the law," the truth of such propositions could not be based upon a correspondence to an objective state of affairs which is completely independent of some subject who makes a judgment about that state of affairs. Whether it is true that the rose is beautiful, it is good to be just, or all men are equal under the law is a question of value and requires the judgment of a person or persons. Beauty, goodness, or equality may not be completely in the "eyes of the beholder" but neither are they solely in the object and completely independent of any observer. Perhaps some believe that God so endowed a rose with beauty that, even if a God and all other observers would cease to exist, the rose would still be beautiful. I have great difficulty in imagining such a situation and even more difficulty imagining that justice is so endowed with goodness or men with equality. All such propositions suppose a subject who imposes value upon that proposition and without whom the value would not be present. Berkeley argued that even the physical universe required a perceiver. Few of us are willing to go that far today, but most of us would agree with someone like Berkeley when it comes to values. Certainly, values have their ultimate basis in the judgments and ideals of some perceiver.

Still, I think there is a place for correspondence as a viable criterion for truth, but in a postmodern age any correspondence concerning anything beyond raw sense data will have to be to another person or persons, and not to objective reality. Any truth claim we make on the basis of correspondence beyond those of brute facts will have to be a correspondence between one's own conceptualization of the world and the conceptualization of some other person or persons. My claim that a particular statement concerning atomic chemistry is true, is only true if it corresponds to the accepted conceptual reality of a community of individuals who adhere to the concepts of atomic chemistry, and therefore observe and understand something similar to what I observe and understand.

It is upsetting to some that the correspondence that establishes truth would be to another person's conceptualization of reality rather than to an objective and independent reality. Christians, as a group, seem among those most upset by the loss of objective reality. I find that strange. One would think that Christians would be quick to recognize that to base their truth in a correspondence to an objective and independent reality borders on idolatry. Indeed, Christians should be among those most receptive to the idea that any truth concerning our conceptualization of the world and its values would have to be based in a correspondence to a person – namely, God. For the Christian, Jesus' statement "I am the ... truth" (John 14:6) can be taken quite literally in that, for the Christian, it is God's conceptualization of the world -- his intentional meaning -- that establishes the ultimate conceptual reality and not things themselves. Thus, for the Christian, truth should be found in a correspondence between our concepts and God's concepts, and not a correspondence to objective reality.

The situation is quite different for an atheistic scientist, who perhaps believes that the conventional concepts of the scientific community are the ultimate reality to which she would have her concepts correspond in order to be true. For a small child, the ultimate conceptual reality may be that of his parents or other family members. For the Marxist, the true conceptual reality is found in yet another person or group of persons.

Certainly, there is nothing in objects that could group them together with other objects. Even though the essential characteristics which serve as a basis for a concept may lie within the brute facts of experience, the selection of those particular characteristics as essential is accomplished by persons who are capable of selecting different essential characteristics and thus conceptualizing things differently.

This fact that we are free to choose whose conceptual reality will be the basis for our correspondence, is not to say that there is no ultimate reality or that whatever anyone chooses as a basis for her correspondence is as good as any other. It is to say, however, that human beings do not have an innate knowledge of whose conceptual reality should serve as a basis for our correspondence. It is not something that is given, but rather it must be chosen. The basis for the choice may vary from one individual to another. Some will choose what seems the most pragmatic concept, while others will choose what seems most coherent. Some may make an emotive choice, while others will choose what they conceive is most beautiful. Still many more will simply choose to accept the concepts that are presented by the dominant culture, but in all cases we choose and have more freedom to do so than we imagine. In fact, we are freer than we would probably like to be, and many of us may wish that the basis for our correspondence was established for us. The reality, however, is that we are free, whether or not we are aware of it and whether or not we like it.

With most of us, this freedom goes unnoticed because we are bombarded, from a very early age, by a host of instructors who pressure us to make their concepts our own. It is easy to succumb to such pressure, and if the community of instructors is large enough, the concepts they attempt to impose upon us can easily be conceived as representing ultimate reality instead of the conceptualization of a particular group of individuals. The larger and more powerful the group, the greater the psychological tyranny which suppresses our freedom to choose alternative conceptualizations. As a matter of fact, as the size and power of the group increases, we easily come to believe that such widely held concepts must correspond to some reality that is more than merely the conceptualizations of other individuals. If the group is large enough, and if we are not aware of other people who conceptualize things differently, we quite naturally think that such concepts are the result of an innate ability to experience and conceptualize the world in that way rather than any other.

The challenge is to resist such pressure and seek instead to come into a correspondence with God's conceptual understanding, rather than the concepts of human beings. For the Christian, ultimate truth is found in a correspondence, not to an ever larger group of people, but to one other person, namely God.

Of course, the central theme of this book has been that God's conceptual understanding is not immediately accessible to human beings, and we are naturally estranged from the very person whose concepts we desire to have as the basis for our correspondence and truth. But to say that we do not know God's intentional meaning is not to say that there is no meaning or that we are not able to overcome our natural estrangement from such meaning. Fortunately, two things allow us to establish a correspondence to God's conceptual understanding. The first is the postmodern insight that has made us aware of the fact that we are not naturally equipped with adequate, God-given concepts. The second is the fact that we have Scripture, which is capable of providing a basis for reconstructing some of the most important concepts God wishes to communicate to us.

Chapter 9

Freedom and Christian Morality

In addition to the concept of truth, the concept of freedom is also essential and foundational to an understanding of postmodern Christianity. Freedom is certainly another concept that needs reconstruction, and, like truth, it is a difficult concept to construct simply by setting forth instances of the concept. However, it can be constructed with the use of biblical instances and certain contemporary insights.

Many today simply deny the existence of human freedom. In the light of what we know about genetics, behavioral conditioning, and sociological pressures, the position that human freedom is an illusion has become popular. The Bible, however, at least implicitly gives evidence of human freedom in that it addresses us as moral agents. If we are indeed moral agents, we must be capable of some sort of choice. Since God's communication to us is intended as a directive or a communication that anticipates a response on our part, there is the obvious implication that those to whom God is speaking are free and capable of responding to his directives.

Of course, the Bible is also explicit about God's sovereignty.

For those God foreknew he also predestined to be conformed to the likeness of
his Son, that he might be the firstborn among many brothers. (Rom. 8:29 NIV)

Thus, for the Christian, human freedom must be conceptualized in the light of
God's sovereignty. But it would seem to be a contradiction for humans to be free and
for God to be sovereign at the same time. If God is sovereign and determines all
things, how can human beings be free? Equally, if human beings are free, then how
could God be truly sovereign? It would seem that God's sovereignty eliminates
human freedom, and human freedom, if it exists, would eliminate God's sovereignty.
But Scripture is quite explicit concerning God's sovereignty while at the same time
it at least implies that we are free. Many people have tried to resolve this
contradiction by redefining freedom or sovereignty. Others have used the
contradiction to show the inconsistency of Scripture. Another possibility involves
questioning the idea of a contradiction and the way it is applied to the question of
human freedom as it stands in the light of God's sovereignty.

Aristotle, who formalized the laws of logic, including the law of contradiction,
thought the law of contradiction was controversial and had to be argued for, which
he did (*Metaphysics* IV, 4). But there have been philosophers from Heraclitus to
Hegel who have leveled powerful arguments against it. Even Plato, in several places
throughout the dialogues – most especially in the *Euthydemus* – demonstrates that the
idea of a contradiction is not so easy to understand. A square circle is certainly a
contradiction, but Socrates can both be a father and not be a father at the same time.

Believing that the law of contradiction was the cornerstone of all thought, Aristotle
was interested in explaining the conditions under which the law of contradiction did
and did not apply. Basically, it applies only to attributes, not to relations. Thus,
Socrates can be a father and not be a father at the same time. He can be a father to
his two sons but not be a father to a dog because the word *father* signifies a relation

rather than an attribute. By contrast, Socrates cannot be over six feet tall and under six feet tall at the same time since that is an attribute rather than a relation.

Additionally, a contradiction occurs only when an attribute is both attributed and not attributed to the same subject at the same time and in the same respect. Aristotle says,

> The same attribute cannot at the same time belong and not belong to the same subject and in the same respect. (Aristotle, *Metaphysics* IV. 3. 18-20)

And,

> It is impossible that contrary attributes should belong at the same time to the same subject . . . . (Aristotle, *Metaphysics* IV. 3. 25-26)

This law of contradiction, however, is not as basic as Aristotle had thought; it is in fact based on another of Aristotle's principles which we had considered earlier concerning the way we formulate our concepts of species or kinds. We will recall that Aristotle suggests that our idea of a species is best conceptualized by uniting the genus of a species with its differentia or the characteristic that differentiates that species from the other members of a particular genus (*Metaphysics* VII. 12. 8-40; *Post. Analytics* II. 13). That is, in order for our concepts to be clear and precise, each concept of a species must be a member of one and only one genus. We conceptualize a living thing as a member of an animal genus or a plant genus, but not both. It may be true that our clearest concepts are those which proceed from, and are members of, a single genus. But while that may be true, the clearest concept is not always the one that best reflects the reality we are attempting to conceptualize. The platypus does not fit neatly into a single genus or more precisely into the class designated as "mammal." Indeed, many species do not seem to fit such a neat Aristotelian model and might better be conceived if we understood them to belong to more than a single genus. As we have seen when addressing the concept of faith, forming concepts according to such an Aristotelian model does not always do justice to our experience of the world or what we find in Scripture. Often it would be more reflective of what we experience to conceptualize certain things as descending from, and being members of, more than a single genus. In the case of faith, we have pointed to a genealogical model of descent rather than the model Aristotle had provided, and here again, with the concept of freedom, a genealogical model seems more appropriate than the Aristotelian one. With a genealogical model, and the idea of descent from multiple genuses, we can conceptualize genuine contradictions and thus better understand the paradoxical concepts God is trying to communicate.

Aristotle, and the Western tradition that followed him, taught us to partition the world through abstract thought. In the analytic tradition, the laws of identity, contradiction, and excluded middle are essential but they lead to a very artificial view of the world. In fact, the world that we encounter in experience and in Scripture is much more paradoxical than the Aristotelian/Enlightenment world that we think about. Of course, we can choose to think about the world differently. Indeed, instead of thinking about the world in terms of an analytic, Aristotelian/Enlightenment model, we could choose to think about it according to a genealogical paradigm. If we understand the world of our experience from a genealogical model, God is not the sole creator of the world. God does, of course, create the brute facts of the world and is sovereign over them, but we do not live in a world of brute facts but in a world where those brute facts have been conceptualized, and the conceptualization of those brute facts are largely the creation of human beings. In Genesis, God creates the world, but Adam names the animals. In this process, the particular name that is associated with a particular group of animals is of little importance. What is important is whether Adam had the ability to form the group to which he applied the name, as God intended them to be grouped, or was he free to make the grouping as he saw fit? As we saw in the first chapter, the way we conceptualize and group the things of our experience does seem to change over time and from one culture to the next. This certainly infers a freedom on our part. Whether that freedom was intended by God, was a result of the fall, or has come about in some other way is hard to say. Though the cause of this freedom might be in doubt, there is no doubt about its reality. We are free to conceptualize at least large portions of our experience as we see fit. Of course, this freedom may be restricted by innate mental and linguistic hardware, as well as our unwillingness to exercise our freedom and to challenge the cultural and historical concepts that attempt to dominate us, but, in spite of these factors, we have a measure of freedom regarding our conceptualization of the world. For some people, that freedom might be limited and amount to no more than the choice of conceptualizing the brute facts of our existence as from the hand of God and meant for our blessing no matter how distasteful they may appear at the moment, or conceptualizing the same brute facts as God's judgment or indifference toward us. Leibniz conceived this to be the extent of human freedom; he believed that God has predetermined all of the perceptions that make up the physical world, but we are nevertheless free. According to Leibniz freedom amounts to no more than volition, a human being's choice to welcome or lament the circumstances God has determined for that individual. This may be a limited view of human freedom, but postmoderns have extended that same freedom to conceptualize far beyond the simple choice of whether to accept our given reality as the "best of all possible worlds" or to conceive it as something other than a blessing from an all-good God.

For a postmodern like Michel Foucault, human beings have an enormous potential freedom to conceptualize the world in a variety of ways. According to Foucault, even if the physical world is beyond our ability to affect, we are free to choose from a variety of competing narratives concerning what the brute facts of the physical world mean and how they are to be conceptualized. We can accept the narrative that our cultural and scientific communities impose upon us, or we can create our own narrative by choosing to look to some other explanation. For Foucault, there have been many different competing narratives that make up history, and we can choose from among them and not merely embrace the dominant cultural view. That view which dominates our culture became the dominant view because of a host of historical, cultural, and political circumstances, not because it is most true or the best way to conceptualize and represent the reality of our existence. Essentially, we face a great variety of different conceptual schemas and philosophies from which to choose. Foucault, like Leibniz, believes we have a freedom concerning what meaning we choose to impose upon the brute facts of our physical existence.

Such a perspective allows us to understand human beings as free concerning their conceptualization of the world, while at the same time God is sovereign over the brute facts of that reality. At this point it may seem that it is in different respects that human beings are both free and not free simultaneously. That is, of course, because we have been taught to think about ourselves and our world according to an analytic model which allows for such abstract thought. In thought, we can separate the conceptual from the brute facts, but in experience the two are inseparable and paradoxically exist within a single reality.

With such a view that human freedom amounts to our liberty to conceptualize large portions of our experience as we wish, liberty will exist in different degrees in different individual. It may be an extensive freedom, as in the case of a postmodern like Foucault, or it may be very limited, as in the case either of Leibniz or one who imagines that our psychological and linguistic hardware is great and far reaching. But in whatever case, we are free to conceptualize, and therein lies the freedom necessary to be moral creatures.

Morality certainly requires freedom, but that freedom need not be an unrestricted freedom to choose the circumstances of our lives. Only a conceptual freedom is necessary because morality, at least in the Christian sense, is not behaviourial. Jesus tells us that the sin is in our hearts and minds.

Ye have heard that it was said by them of old time, thou shalt not commit adultery. But I say unto you, That whosoever looketh on a woman to lust after her hath committed adultery with her already in his heart. (Matt. 5:27-28 KJV)

Jesus also says something similar about anger and equates it with murder (Matt.

5:21-22). Equally, John confirms that teaching: "Whosoever hateth his brother is a murderer" (1 John 3:15 KJV).

Furthermore, in addition to sin existing within our hearts and minds, righteousness, for the Christian, is equally a matter of our hearts and minds. That is not to say that in order to be righteous we must achieve a purity of heart and mind. That is not the idea of Christian righteousness. The ideal of Christian morality is not that we would be able to avoid all sin, but that we would confess our sins and repent, in order that Jesus would forgive our sins. For the Christian, righteousness means to be forgiven, not to be guiltless. We might not have a freedom over the world of brute facts, even including our own actions, but we do have the liberty to agree with Jesus and conceptualize sin as he does. This is a choice over which we are free. We may choose to conceptualize our thoughts and feelings as sin, and repent of them, or we can disagree with Jesus and choose to conceptualize such thoughts and feelings in some other way.

This is the Scriptural view of sin and righteousness, but few of us make it our own perspective. We tend to side with the dominant cultural view that sin and injustice only exist when they are external and involve others. Our judicial system punishes bad behavior, not bad thoughts. Even Plato, who was concerned with the internal condition of the soul and the harm injustice does to that soul, did not think that injustice done in the imagination was harmful to anyone, including the person who imagines doing such injustice. This is well illustrated at the beginning of the second book of Plato's *Republic*, where Glaucon challenges Socrates' idea of justice, with a myth concerning the ancestor of Gyges, the Lydian. The story is that Gyges' ancestor was a shepherd who one day after a great deluge and earthquake noticed a chasm where he was shepherding. Upon entering the chasm, he found a great hollow bronze horse which contained a corpse that seemed to be of greater than human stature. The corpse had a gold ring on its hand which Gyges' ancestor took before returning to the outer world. In wearing the ring, he noticed that when he turned the collet or face of the ring in toward his palm, he became invisible. Upon turning the ring the other way, he would reappear. With this power to become invisible at will, the shepherd had acquired the power to do injustice and not suffer for it. With this power, he chose to seduce the king's wife and kill the king in order to take his kingdom.

Now I have never understood how being invisible enabled him to seduce the king's wife, but the idea that Glaucon is painting is of a man who can do injustice and have the power not to suffer for it. Glaucon's claim is that such a man with the power to do injustice and avoid punishment would always choose to do injustice. He says imagine that there were two such rings, one being given to the just man and the other to the unjust man. Glaucon claims that both men will succumb and will do injustice. Glaucon might be right: given the power, we would all choose to do injustice.

Of course, Plato doesn't care about what all men will do but rather what they should do. And what men should do is to resist the desire to do injustice even if they had the power to do the injustice with immunity. His reasoning is that the doing of injustice harms one's self. In particular, it harms the internal condition of one's soul, and therefore it should be avoided.

To Plato, the great evil of Athenian society was that they followed Homer in believing that human excellence amounted to excess. A great man or woman is one who has more than others and is better able to indulge one's desire or appetite for pleasure. Many of us today would still agree with that idea of the human excellence, or at least we act as if we agree with such a view. Of course, Plato opposed such a view, believing that excessive pleasure leads to the destruction of the soul. This is a major theme that runs throughout the dialogues. According to Plato, we can only have as much pleasure and indulge our appetite to the extent that we have wisdom to control that appetite or desire. A desire for pleasure without wisdom to control it brings destruction rather than virtue to the soul. To Plato, the virtuous soul is the result of each part of the soul – namely, appetite, spirit, and reason – functioning properly and being in harmony with each other. Appetite functioning properly produces the virtue of temperance; spirit functioning properly and being neither excessive nor deficient produces courage; and reason controlling appetite and spirit neither too much nor too little produces wisdom. Justice is the fourth virtue and results from the three parts of the soul functioning in harmony together. So, as in the just city where each part of the city must function and be in harmony with the other parts, there must be the same harmony in the soul of the just person. In the *Phaedrus*, Plato pictures the soul as a chariot with reason as the charioteer, and spirit and appetite as the two horses that the charioteer must either hold back or urge on. Appetite is pictured as an especially wild horse and must constantly be held back.

Certainly, a universal human problem is the threat of being led by an unbridled desire for one pleasure or another. Plato's solution to the problem is to have all of our desires or appetites under the tight control of reason. For Plato, the ring of Gyges would add to the problem rather than serve as the solution. A ring of Gyges would allow our appetite to be ever more excessive and thus more difficult to keep under the control of reason. If my ability to indulge my desire for pleasure is limited, it is easier for reason to keep appetite under control. But if my ability to indulge my desires increases, it becomes more difficult to bring appetite under the control of reason. Thus, the ring of Gyges would tend to pervert the proper function of the soul by giving more power and opportunity for appetite and spirit (but especially appetite) to dominate over reason. Such a ring would tend to produce a more bestial nature, over which appetite and spirit ruled, rather than the nature Plato envisioned with reason in control.

This certainly seems to be the case, and an increase in empowerment most often leads to destruction rather than virtue. Imagine being given a huge sum of money when young and before reason really had a chance to fully develop. Would such a bequest prove a blessing or a curse? From my own perspective, poverty was an enormous blessing in that it kept me from excessive pleasure in my youth.

Of course, in the case of the ring of Gyges, the temptation involves not merely being able to afford more pleasure, but being able to acquire more pleasure unjustly because there is no fear of suffering for the injustice one does. For Plato, however, it would seem that the harm is in the acquisition of excessive pleasure rather than the doing of injustice, for it is this acquisition that stimulates the appetite to the point of being out of control and not the fact that pleasure was acquired unjustly. Indulging appetite beyond the control of reason brings harm to the soul, whether it is done justly or unjustly.

Also, from this Platonic perspective, the intent to do injustice brings no harm to the soul so long as it is only imagined and does not stimulate appetite beyond the control of reason. This is perhaps why Plato never seems to see the imagination as the equivalent of the ring of Gyges – but of course it is. With our imagination, as with the ring of Gyges, we are able to do all manner of injustice in order to increase our pleasure because we have immunity from suffering for our imagined acts of adultery, revenge, or perverse cruelty. Though I may refrain from actually doing injustice because of the punishment or retribution I would suffer if I did do such things, I have immunity in my imagination, just as I would if I had the ring of Gyges. In my imagination, I am free to take pleasure in doing all sorts of injustice without fear of retaliation or punishment, and I do.

Although he is concerned with the internal condition of the soul, Plato, however, sees little harm in imagined injustice and the pleasure it brings. If he did believe that such imagined actions were harmful to the soul, he never mentions it in his lengthy response to Glaucon. In fact, neither Socrates nor any other character in the dialogues ever mentions the imagination bringing direct damage to the soul the way a ring of Gyges does by allowing us to indulge in excess pleasure. The perversion of the Platonic nature seems to occur only when excess pleasure becomes a reality. For Plato, it must be that imagined pleasures do not stimulate the appetite to the point that it would threaten reason the way actual pleasures do. Plato's picture must be one in which appetite becomes uncontrollable only when there is a greater possibility of actual pleasures being realized; otherwise, he would condemn our appetite for imagined pleasures as well as actual ones.

Most of us today would agree with Plato. Our judicial system only considers actual injustice, and people are not held responsible for what they merely think. Our culture maintains that the breaking of law does not occur in the imagination, and our imagined acts of murder or adultery are not damaging either to others or ourselves, just as the imagined consumption of large quantities of illegal drugs harms neither others nor ourselves. Our culture has certainly agreed with Plato on this point, but Jesus has something different to say on this matter. Jesus tells us that sin, including all the damage that comes with sin, comes not merely with the act but with the thought.

Indeed, from the Christian perspective, the imagination both gives us the power to do real injustice and the ability to do real harm to the soul. It brings harm to the soul for the same reason that Plato believed the doing of injustice brought harm to the soul, by providing a power to the individual that allows him to pervert the very nature and function of the soul. Of course, for Plato that meant giving more power to appetite, thus making it more difficult for reason to control the bestial side of our nature.

For the Christian, however, the perversion of the soul is different. Indeed, for the Christian, the nature and function of the soul is to love and worship God. The fulfillment of that nature and purpose begins and ends in our imagination. Equally, our rebellion, whereby we love and worship other things before God, exists first and foremost in our imagination as well.

Thus, just as the ring of Gyges gives us a power that is contrary to our nature and perverts what Plato says is the nature of our soul, the imagination does the same to the Christian notion of the soul. As the ring of Gyges enables its wearer to develop a nature that is contrary to the reason governed nature Plato envisioned, the imagination allows us to pervert the nature God intends for us.

The Christian notion of sin is, as it was for Plato, an offense against our own nature, not an offense to God's ego. The reason sin offends God is because of his love and concern for us. Pitiful creatures such as ourselves could have no effect upon an all-powerful God if he did not love and care for us to the extent that he would be hurt when we do harm to ourselves.

Unlike Plato, however, the Christian notion of sin extends to the imagination because it is in our thoughts that our character is formed and it is there that it is perverted. The Christian picture of human nature is not one in which reason must rule over appetite, but one in which love and service to God must rule over love and service to ourselves. For the Christian, the perversion of our nature occurs long before we indulge some actual pleasure which stimulates appetite beyond the control of reason. It begins when our imagination sets itself on things other than God and what he has for our lives.

In a similar way, righteousness exists for the Christian in the imagination as well. Indeed, the righteous one, as God conceives him, is not someone who has all of his behavior under the control of reason, as Plato and most of us imagine, but one who comes to repentance and accepts the forgiveness Jesus has provided. If we accept this biblical view of sin and repentance, the freedom we need to be moral agents is not the liberty to choose to do the right thing, but the ability to conceptualize sin as God does and repent. It is an internal freedom which has little to do with the brute facts of the external world and everything to do with the internal conceptual world within which we are free. Righteousness for the Christian amounts to no more than our conceptualizing the world, and our place in it, as God does. That is, we come to see our need for a savior, and we surrender to his sovereign grace.

Beyond our initial conceptualization of ourselves as sinners who need a savior, the Christian life continues to be largely conceptual rather than behavioral. Our righteousness comes through a repentance which is certainly conceptual, but God also desires to make us ever more into the image of his son. The process by which we are made into that image is also largely conceptual. It is not that we act like Jesus, but that we think like him and have his understanding – his heart and mind.

All of God's chosen are predestined to be conformed to the image of his son (Rom. 8:29), but our being made into his image is certainly a process. Our willingness to have our minds renewed and our concepts reformed by Scripture is certainly one of the factors which determines how much of his likeness we attain.

Hence, the apparent contradiction with which we began this chapter is, in fact, not a contradiction between God's sovereignty and human freedom, but rather a contradiction within the very nature of a human being. Indeed, our nature is made up of both the brute facts of our animal existence (over which God is sovereign), as well as the fact that we have an enormous liberty concerning how we are to conceptualize such facts. Thus, we are both determined and free at the same time. We are both of an animal genus and without freedom (Job 25:6), but also we have a potential to create our own world since we are made *imago dei* (Gen. 5:1) and have been endowed with the freedom of a creative being.

Of course, we may avoid this contradiction if we imagine that we have two separate natures or that we live in two separate worlds. But this solution does not reflect the reality of our experience. The truth is that we are of one nature and we live in one world. We may be able to think about ourselves or our world as two but we experience them as one. Indeed, our experience is singular but it does contain a genuine contradiction since we descend from, and are members of, two different genuses.

In our thinking we find contradictions intolerable and attempt to eliminate them, but that is only because our thinking is fashioned after a mathematical and material model. According to such a model, the law of contradiction holds. Something cannot be seven and not be seven at the same time and in the same respect, nor can two physical objects occupy the same space at the same time. But the mathematical/material model does not engulf the whole of reality. With another model two very different and apparently contradictory things can be present in the same space, at the same time, and in the same respect. In music, two very different notes can fill the same space at the same time. Should our understanding of human freedom follow the mathematical/material model or the musical model? Of course, the prejudice of our culture favors the mathematical/material model. A conceptual understanding based upon that model, however, makes it difficult to understand our own nature from a Scriptural perspective. Indeed, Scripture not only implies that human beings are both free and not free, but it equally seems to point to the fact that human beings are members of two very different genuses. It is thus possible to conceptualize our nature as possessing a freedom which we have inherited by being a member of one genus and an absence of freedom which we have inherited by being members of another genus. It is not that in some respects we are free and in other respects not free, or that at one moment we are free and at another not. If our nature is understood as having a genealogical descent from two very different genuses, one can conceive that we are in the same respect free and not free simultaneously.

Chapter 10

Postscript

Modernity propagated the idea that knowledge should be objective and mathematically precise. Under that influence, biblical exegetes sought an ever more narrow and precise understanding of Scripture. Today, postmoderns deconstruct texts, and literary theorists tell us that the author's intentional meaning is unknowable. Of course, deconstruction and a loss of authorial meaning follows from the Enlightenment quest to achieve a knowledge that is objective and mathematically precise. It is only by supposing the narrow and precise Enlightenment concepts of meaning that deconstruction can take place and authorial intent can be lost. What makes it possible to deconstruct a text or to show that it is not possible to know the author's intentional meaning is the supposition that the concepts to which words refer must be like mathematical concepts – tied down, precise, and univocal. Given such a supposition, it is then easy to show that our concepts are not of such a nature, and therefore meaning is impossible. But the truth is that meaning, especially authorial meaning, is not dependent upon narrow and univocal concepts after the model of mathematics. Meaningful and communicable concepts need not be like those narrow and precise concepts we have been told must be at the base of our understanding.

Modernity taught us to seek ever more precise essences and definitions after the model of mathematics, but, in order to know other persons, what we need are broader concepts which might better reflect the fullness and richness of their intentional meaning. My wife often shares her conceptual understanding with me – an understanding that is never narrow and precise because her concepts themselves are not like the artificial concepts that modernity tried to convince us were so essential to human understanding. The situation is similar with God and the communication of his conceptual understanding.

Given this insight that our concepts need not be narrow or precise in order to be meaningful and communicable, it should be clear that authorial intent is able to be communicated, even when the author's concepts are radically different than those of our language community. In spite of the fact that the words God uses to communicate to us are the product of, and ultimately rooted in, human judgment and do not necessarily reflect God's intentional meaning, God is still able to communicate his intentional meaning, if we understand that his concepts do not follow the narrow and precise model set by mathematics. Indeed, they are much broader and richer than the concepts recommended by the sciences of modernity. In fact, they more closely resemble the kind of personal concepts that individuals often share with those people with whom they are intimate. Such personal concepts are not limited to a single, narrow definition or meaning, but are multifarious and are communicated, not with a single definition or *eidos*, but with repeated examples that reflect a myriad of dimensions and aspects which produce in us an understanding that is different from the kind of understanding engendered by mathematics. This seems to be the nature of the concepts that God is trying to communicate to us. They are intelligible, and they bring us to know God in a deep and rich way, but they are certainly not the kind of concepts that modernity set forth as the model for human understanding. Hence, God is able to communicate to us, and he is able to communicate well; what he cannot do is to communicate to us in the limited way that modernity would want.

Some people may think that such a broadening of our concepts causes them to lose, rather than gain, meaning, but they believe that because of an analytic legacy begun with Aristotle and made mathematical with the Enlightenment. But concepts need not be narrow and precise in order to be meaningful.

This book has been an attempt to show how we might begin to move toward broader and richer concepts, rather than more narrow ones. Such a broadening of our concepts should not affect the basic truths of Christianity, since the basic truths of Christianity do not require any special understanding of God's peculiar intentional meaning. We all enter into the Christian life with a very rough understanding. Only after we have accepted the basic truths of Christianity, with a faith that is initially little more than hope, do we come to a place of needing to better understand what God means when he tells us that we are to love our wives as Christ loves the church (Eph. 5:25), or that we are to live by faith (Rom. 1:17). It is here that we need to know more fully what he is trying to communicate, and it is here that our concepts must become broader, not more narrow. An ever greater understanding of God's intentional meaning is not necessary for us to enter the Christian life, but it is necessary for us to become more perfect and obedient servants.

Furthermore, if we can come to understand that we will never know God's intentional meaning with the kind of exactness that modernity set as the goal for human understanding, and that such a goal in many respects was ill-conceived, we might at long last put an end to much of what has kept Christians apart for so long. Christians have been primarily separated by their belief that human beings are capable of understanding God's intentional meaning in an exact and precise way after the model provided by mathematics. If, however, God's concepts are rich, personal concepts that defy such a narrow understanding, then much of the basis for our separation is lost. Without precise and narrow concepts after the mathematical model, I can no longer maintain that my understanding is correct to the exclusion of all other possible understandings. If God's concepts follow the model of personal rather than mathematical concepts, then we are forced to concede that we only know in part, or "through a glass darkly" (1 Cor. 13:12KJV). By understanding that the words of Scripture do not refer to the kind of precise and narrow concepts that modernity sought, we are forced to accept what a colleague of mine refers to as "humble hermeneutics." Unlike the hermeneutics of modernity, the "humble hermeneutics" of a postmodern age offer the enormous benefit of reducing our confidence in our own understanding, thereby making possible the kind of unity God desires for his church.

Works Cited

Aristotle. *Metaphysics. The Basic Works of Aristotle.* Ed. Richard Mckeon. New York: Random House, 1941. 681-926.

- - - . *Posterior Analytics. The Basic Works of Aristotle.* Ed. Richard Mckeon. New York: Random House, 1941. 108-86.

Berkeley, George. *The Principle of Human Knowledge.* Ed. T. E. Jessop. Camden, NJ: Thomas Nelson, 1950. Vol. 2 of *The Works of George Berkeley.* Ed. A. A. Luce and T. E. Jessop.

Crabb, Larry. *Men and Women: Enjoying the Difference.* Grand Rapids: Zondervan, 1991.

Descartes, Rene. *Discourse on the Method. Philosophical Works of Descartes.* Trans. Elizabeth S. Haldane and G. R. T. Ross. New York: Dover, 1955. 1:81-130.

Edwards, Jonathan. *The End for Which God Created the World. God's Passion for His Glory.* Ed. John Piper. Wheaton, IL: Crossway Books, 1998. 125-251.

- - - . *The Religious Affections.* Carlisle, PA: The Banner of Truth Trust, 1997.

Foucault, Michel. "Nietzsche, Genealogy, History." Twentieth Century Continental Philosophy. Ed. Todd May. Trans. Donald F. Bouchard and Sherry Simon. Upper Saddle River, NJ: Prentice Hall, 1997. 233-50.

Gadamer, Hans-Georg. *Philosophical Hermeneutics.* Trans. David E. Linge. Berkeley, CA: U of California, 1976.

Gray, John. *Men Are from Mars, Women Are from Venus.* New York: Harper Collins, 1992.

Guyon, Jeanne. *Experiencing the Depths of Jesus Christ.* Sargent, GA: Seed Sowers, 1975.

Hume, David. *An Inquiry Concerning Human Understanding.* Ed. Charles W. Hendel. Upper Saddle River, NJ: Prentice Hall, 1995.

- - - . *A Treatise of Human Nature.* Ed. L. A. Selby-Bigge. New York: Oxford UP, 1985.

Kierkegaard, Soren. *Fear and Trembling.* Trans. Walter Lowrie. Princeton, NJ: Princeton UP, 1970.

Landesman, Charles. "Does Language Embody a Philosophical Point of View?" *The Review of Metaphysics*. 14. (1961): 617-36.

Lawrence, Brother. *The Practice of the Presence of God.* Uhrichsville, OH: Barbour and Company, Inc., 1993.

Leibniz, Gottfried Wilhelm. *Monadology*. *Monadology and Other Philosophical Essays*. Trans. Paul Schrecker and Anne Martin Schrecker. New York: Macmillan, 1965.

Livingston, Donald W. *Philosophical Melancholy and Delirium: Hume's Pathology of Philosophy*. Chicago: U of Chicago, 1998.

Locke, John. *An Essay Concerning Human Understanding*. 1689. Ed. Peter H. Nidditch. Oxford: Oxford UP, 1975.

Miller, Perry. *Jonathan Edwards*. Toronto: William Sloan Associates, 1949.

Ortega y Gasset, Jose. "Falling in Love." Trans. Toby Talbot. *On Love and Friendship*. Ed. Clifford Williams. Boston: Jones and Bartlett, 1995.

Piper, John. *God's Passion for His Glory*. Wheaton, IL: Crossway Books, 1998.

Plato. *Euthydemus*. Trans. W. H. D. Rouse. *The Collected Dialogues of Plato*. Ed. Edith Hamilton and Huntington Cairns. Princeton, NJ: Princeton UP, 1989. 385-420.

- - - . *Meno*. Trans. W. K. C. Guthrie. *The Collected Dialogues of Plato*. Ed. Edith Hamilton and Huntington Cairns. Princeton, NJ: Princeton UP, 1989. 353-84.

- - - . *The Republic*. Trans. Paul Shorey. *The Collected Dialogues of Plato*. Ed. Edith Hamilton and Huntington Cairns. Princeton, NJ: Princeton UP, 1989. 526-74.

- - - . *Symposium*. Trans. Michael Joyce. *The Collected Dialogues of Plato*. Ed. Edith Hamilton and Huntington Cairns. Princeton, NJ: Princeton UP, 1989. 526-74.

- - - . *Theaetetus*. Trans. F. M. Cornford. *The Collected Dialogues of Plato*. Ed. Edith Hamilton and Huntington Cairns. Princeton, NJ: Princeton UP, 1989. 845-919.

Slupik, Chris. "A New Interpretation of Hume's 'Of Miracles.'" *Religious Studies.* 31.4 (1995): 517-36.

Tannen, Deborah. *You Just Don't Understand: Women and Men in Conversation.* New York: Ballantine, 1990.

Wittgenstein, Ludwig. *The Blue and Brown Books.* New York: Harper and Row, 1965.

- - - . *Philosophical Investigations.* Trans. G. E. M. Anscombe. New York: MacMillan, 1968.